# DIABETIC RENAL DIET

## COOKBOOK FOR BEGINNERS

DR. HERMIONE MENDEZ

**2000** days of recipes

**100+** diabetes and kidney-friendly meals

**30-DAY MEAL PLAN**

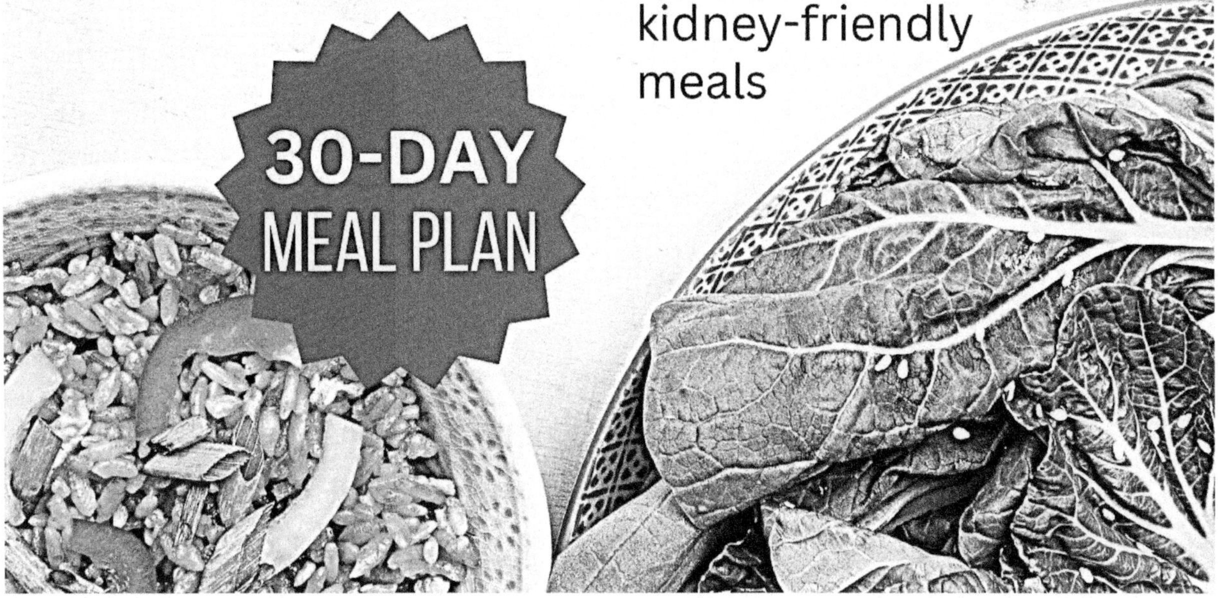

# DIABETIC RENAL DIET FOR BEGINNERS

The Complete Low-Salt, Low-Sugar, Low Potassium, And Low-Phosphorus Diet To Reversing Diabetes and Kidney Disease With Easy Cooking.

DR. HERMIONE MENDEZ

## Copyright © 2023 HERMIONE MENDEZ

All rights reserved.

No part of this publication may be reproduced, distributed, or transmitted in any form or by any means, including photocopying, recording, or other electronic or mechanical methods, without the prior written permission of the copyright holder, except in the case of brief quotations embodied in critical reviews and certain other noncommercial uses permitted by copyright law.

The content of this publication may not be modified, adapted, or used for commercial purposes without prior written permission from the copyright holder.

# TABLE OF CONTENTS

Introduction .................................................................................................. 11

**Chapter 1: Understanding Diabetes and Renal Disease** ................... 15
- Diabetes: Types, Causes, and Management ........................................ 15
- Renal Disease: Causes, Stages, and Treatment ................................... 16
- The Relationship Between Diabetes and Renal Disease .................... 17

**Chapter 2: Principles of the Diabetic Renal Diet** ............................ 19
- Overview of the Diabetic Renal Diet: A Journey Towards Balance and Wellness ................................................................................................ 19
- Balancing Blood Sugar and Kidney Health: A Delicate Dance .......... 19
- Importance of Nutrient Control and Portion Management: Building a Solid Foundation .................................................................................. 20
- Embracing Emotional Transformation: Nurturing Your Well-Being . 21

**Chapter 3: Essential Nutrients for Diabetic Renal Diets** ................. 23
- Carbohydrates and Blood Sugar Control: ........................................... 23
- Protein and Kidney Function: ............................................................. 24
- Sodium, Potassium, and Fluid Balance: .............................................. 24
- Phosphorus and Calcium Management: ............................................. 25
- Embracing the Journey: ...................................................................... 26

## Chapter 4: Meal Planning for Diabetes and Renal Disease ............ 29
Creating a Balanced Plate ............................................................. 29
Glycemic Index and Blood Sugar Impact ..................................... 30
Recommended Daily Intake of Sodium, Potassium, Phosphorus, Calcium, and Sugar in Diabetic Renal Patients ........................... 30
Sample Meal Plans for Different Caloric Needs ........................... 32

## Chapter 5: Smart Shopping for Diabetic Renal Diets ..................... 35
Reading Food Labels and Making Informed Choices ................... 35
Grocery Shopping Tips for Diabetes and Renal Health ................ 36
Building a Diabetic Renal-Friendly Pantry ................................... 38

## Chapter 6: Cooking Techniques and Tips for Diabetic Renal Diets. 41
Healthy Cooking Methods for Kidney-Friendly Meals ................. 41
Reducing Sodium and Enhancing Flavors .................................... 43
Meal Preparation and Batch Cooking ........................................... 44

## Chapter 7: Breakfasts to Start the Day Right ................................. 47
## Chapter 8: Satisfying Soups and Salads ........................................ 67
## Chapter 9: Wholesome Main Dishes ............................................. 87
## Chapter 10: Delicious Sides and Snacks ..................................... 115
## Chapter 11: Delectable Desserts for Diabetic Renal Diets ........... 133

## Bonus Chapter: Beverages and Refreshing Drinks ..........................157

- Recipe: Cucumber Mint Infused Water .................................................157
- Recipe: Fresh Lemonade (using sugar substitutes)..............................157
- Recipe: Hibiscus Iced Tea (unsweetened) ............................................158
- Recipe: Berry Blast Smoothie (made with low-potassium fruits like berries and almond milk)......................................................................159
- Recipe: Green Tea with Lemon (unsweetened).................................160
- Recipe: Watermelon Lime Slushie (using sugar substitutes) .............161
- Recipe: Ginger Turmeric Detox Water ................................................162
- Recipe: Sparkling Water with a Splash of Fresh Lime Juice .............163
- Recipe: Iced Herbal Tea with Stevia....................................................164
- Recipe: Coconut Water (low in potassium) ........................................164
- Recipe: Pineapple Ginger Cooler (using sugar substitutes) .............165
- Recipe: Unsweetened Almond Milk Latte..........................................166
- Recipe: Cranberry Spritzer (using unsweetened cranberry juice) .....167
- Recipe: Peppermint Iced Mocha (using sugar substitutes and unsweetened cocoa)..............................................................................168
- Recipe: Herbal Iced Tea Blend (using kidney-safe herbs like chamomile and rooibos)........................................................................................169
- Recipe: Sparkling Cucumber Limeade ...............................................170
- Recipe: Minty Fresh Green Smoothie (made with low-potassium greens like spinach).........................................................................................171
- Recipe: Blueberry Basil Lemonade (using sugar substitutes) ...........172
- Recipe: Water with a Twist of Fresh Citrus (orange, grapefruit, or lime) ................................................................................................................173
- Recipe: Iced Decaf Coffee with Sugar-Free Syrup............................174

## 30-Day Diabetic Renal Meal Plan ..................................................... 175
### Day 1: ............................................................................................. 175
### Day 2: ............................................................................................. 175
### Day 3: ............................................................................................. 175
### Day 4: ............................................................................................. 175
### Day 5: ............................................................................................. 176
### Day 6: ............................................................................................. 176
### Day 7: ............................................................................................. 176
### Day 8: ............................................................................................. 177
### Day 9: ............................................................................................. 177
### Day 10: ........................................................................................... 177
### Day 11: ........................................................................................... 177
### Day 12: ........................................................................................... 178
### Day 13: ........................................................................................... 178
### Day 14: ........................................................................................... 178
### Day 15: ........................................................................................... 179
### Day 16: ........................................................................................... 179
### Day 17: ........................................................................................... 179
### Day 18: ........................................................................................... 179
### Day 19: ........................................................................................... 180
### Day 20: ........................................................................................... 180
### Day 21: ........................................................................................... 180
### Day 22: ........................................................................................... 181
### Day 23: ........................................................................................... 181
### Day 24: ........................................................................................... 181
### Day 25: ........................................................................................... 181

Day 26: ....................................................................................... 182
Day 27: ....................................................................................... 182
Day 28: ....................................................................................... 182
Day 29: ....................................................................................... 183
Day 30: ....................................................................................... 183

## Chapter 13: Dining Out and Special Occasions ............................. 185

Navigating Restaurant Menus ....................................................... 185

Tips for Eating Out with Diabetes and Renal Disease ...................... 186

Modifying Recipes for Special Occasions ........................................ 187

## Chapter 14: Lifestyle Tips for Diabetes and Kidney Health ............ 189

Regular Physical Activity and Its Benefits ....................................... 189

Stress Management Techniques .................................................... 190

Monitoring Blood Sugar and Kidney Function ................................ 191

## Recommended Reading ............................................................. 193

## Conclusion .................................................................................. 199

## Appendix .................................................................................... 201

Diabetic Renal Diet Substitutions Guide: ....................................... 201

Cooking Techniques for Diabetic and Renal-Friendly Meals: .......... 202

Frequently Asked Questions: ........................................................ 203

# INTRODUCTION

As a compassionate doctor who has witnessed the struggles of countless patients battling diabetes and renal disease, my heart aches for those enduring the challenging combination of these conditions. I have seen firsthand the devastating impact they can have, with diabetes often leading to kidney failure, robbing individuals of their vitality and well-being. These experiences have ignited a fire within me, compelling me to delve deeper into the intricate link between diabetes and renal disease and to help my patients discover effective ways to manage and combat these health challenges.

Welcome to my cookbook, the Diabetic Renal Diet, where I, Dr. Hermione Mendez, share my extensive knowledge accumulated over two decades as a practicing physician. I am thrilled to embark on this journey with you and offer insights into the critical importance of maintaining a nourishing diet for those grappling with diabetes and renal issues.

Throughout my career, I have witnessed the profound impact that diabetes and renal disease can have on individuals and their loved ones. I have witnessed the toll it takes on families, relationships, and overall quality of life. However, amidst these struggles, I have also been witness to the incredible resilience and determination displayed by patients who refuse to allow these conditions to define them.

One of the most disheartening aspects of managing diabetes and renal disease is the overwhelming lack of clear and concise information available to patients. I have seen firsthand the confusion and frustration that stems from conflicting advice received from healthcare professionals, family members, and friends. Many individuals face immense challenges when trying to find healthy and delectable meals that align with their dietary restrictions, while others simply do not know where to begin their journey.

It was precisely these challenges that served as the catalyst for the creation of this cookbook. I yearned to provide patients with a comprehensive resource that would empower them to take control of their health and elevate their quality of life. My aim was to fashion a guide that would simplify the path to adhering to a diabetic renal diet. Through this cookbook, I endeavor to present you with recipes that are not only healthy and nutritious, but also mouthwatering and easily prepared. I firmly believe that food should be a source of joy, and with the right recipes at your disposal, you can relish in delicious meals while upholding a healthy lifestyle. My sincerest hope is that this cookbook will serve as a guiding light for those struggling to manage their diabetes and renal disease, illuminating their path toward a brighter, healthier future.

Within the pages of this book, you will discover a diverse array of recipes that are as tantalizing as they are beneficial for your well-being. These recipes have been meticulously crafted to cater to the specific dietary needs of individuals contending with diabetes and renal disease. They are designed to be effortlessly prepared, incorporating ingredients readily available at your local grocery store.

However, this cookbook goes beyond a mere collection of recipes; it is a holistic guide to embracing a healthier way of life for those navigating the complexities of diabetes and renal disease. Within these pages, you will find not only a plethora of delectable recipes spanning breakfast to dinner and everything in between, but also valuable tips and tricks for managing your condition. I will provide insights on how to seamlessly integrate healthy eating into your everyday routine, making it a sustainable and enjoyable lifestyle choice.

As you embark on this culinary adventure, I fervently hope that this cookbook will serve as an invaluable resource, guiding you through the intricate landscape of diabetic renal diets. Together, we will traverse this path towards improved health and well-being, empowering you to lead a more vibrant and joyous life. With great enthusiasm, let us embark on this transformative journey together. So, without further ado, let us commence this flavorful odyssey!

# CHAPTER 1: UNDERSTANDING DIABETES AND RENAL DISEASE

## DIABETES: TYPES, CAUSES, AND MANAGEMENT

Diabetes is a complex metabolic disorder characterized by elevated blood glucose levels due to either insufficient insulin production or ineffective utilization of insulin by the body. There are two primary types of diabetes: type 1 and type 2.

Type 1 diabetes, also known as insulin-dependent diabetes mellitus (IDDM), is an autoimmune disease in which the body's immune system mistakenly attacks and destroys the insulin-producing cells in the pancreas. This results in a lack of insulin, requiring individuals with type 1 diabetes to rely on insulin injections or insulin pumps to manage their blood sugar levels.

Type 2 diabetes, also referred to as non-insulin dependent diabetes mellitus (NIDDM), is the most common form of diabetes, accounting for approximately 90-95% of all cases. It is characterized by insulin resistance, meaning the body's cells do not respond effectively to insulin. Over time, the pancreas may struggle to produce enough insulin to compensate, leading to high blood sugar levels.

The causes of diabetes are multifactorial and can involve genetic predisposition, environmental factors, lifestyle choices, and obesity. While type 1 diabetes is often diagnosed in childhood or early adulthood and is not preventable, type 2 diabetes is largely preventable or manageable through lifestyle modifications, including a healthy diet, regular exercise, weight management, and medication if necessary.

## RENAL DISEASE: CAUSES, STAGES, AND TREATMENT

Renal disease, also known as kidney disease, refers to the impairment or damage to the kidneys' structure and function. The kidneys play a vital role in maintaining overall health by filtering waste products, excess fluids, and toxins from the blood, regulating electrolyte balance, and producing hormones that influence blood pressure and red blood cell production.

Chronic kidney disease (CKD) is a progressive condition that develops over time and is characterized by a gradual loss of kidney function. Common causes of CKD include diabetes, hypertension (high blood pressure), glomerulonephritis (inflammation of the kidney's filtering units), and polycystic kidney disease (an inherited disorder).

CKD is typically classified into five stages based on the estimated glomerular filtration rate (eGFR), which measures the kidneys' filtering capacity. In the early stages, symptoms may be minimal or absent, making regular screening and monitoring crucial for early detection and intervention.

Treatment options for renal disease depend on the underlying cause and the stage of kidney disease. Lifestyle modifications such as dietary changes (e.g., reduced sodium and protein intake), blood pressure management, and blood sugar control are essential in slowing the progression of kidney damage. Medications, including angiotensin-converting enzyme inhibitors (ACE inhibitors) or angiotensin receptor blockers (ARBs), may be prescribed to help manage blood pressure and protect kidney function.

In advanced stages of CKD, when kidney function declines significantly, renal replacement therapies such as hemodialysis, peritoneal dialysis, or kidney transplantation may be necessary to sustain life.

## THE RELATIONSHIP BETWEEN DIABETES AND RENAL DISEASE

Diabetes and renal disease often go hand in hand, and the relationship between the two is bidirectional. Diabetes is a leading cause of chronic kidney disease, accounting for approximately 30-40% of all cases of end-stage renal disease (ESRD). The presence of high blood sugar levels over an extended period can damage the small blood vessels and filters in the kidneys, impairing their ability to function properly.

Conversely, renal disease can also contribute to the development and progression of diabetes. The kidneys play a crucial role in insulin metabolism and clearance from the bloodstream. When kidney function is impaired, insulin sensitivity may be affected, leading to insulin resistance and elevated blood sugar levels.

The coexistence of diabetes and renal disease poses significant challenges in managing both conditions effectively. Individuals with diabetes and renal disease require close monitoring of blood glucose levels, blood pressure control, and adherence to dietary restrictions, including limiting protein and sodium intake. Medications may need to be adjusted to ensure optimal management of both conditions while considering potential interactions and side effects.

It is essential for individuals with diabetes and renal disease to work closely with a multidisciplinary healthcare team, including endocrinologists, nephrologists, registered dietitians, and diabetes educators, to develop a comprehensive treatment plan. Regular medical check-ups, laboratory tests, and ongoing education are crucial components of managing these conditions and maintaining overall health.

By understanding the intricate relationship between diabetes and renal disease, individuals can make informed decisions, implement lifestyle modifications, and follow medical advice to mitigate the risks, slow disease progression, and improve their quality of life.

# CHAPTER 2: PRINCIPLES OF THE DIABETIC RENAL DIET

## OVERVIEW OF THE DIABETIC RENAL DIET: A JOURNEY TOWARDS BALANCE AND WELLNESS

Imagine embarking on a journey where you not only take control of your blood sugar levels but also nurture the health of your kidneys. Welcome to the world of the Diabetic Renal Diet, a path that intertwines the principles of diabetes management and kidney health, guiding you towards a state of balance and wellness. This chapter serves as your compass, illuminating the importance of this specialized diet and providing you with the knowledge and tools to embark on this emotional and transformative journey.

## BALANCING BLOOD SUGAR AND KIDNEY HEALTH: A DELICATE DANCE

As someone living with diabetes, you are already familiar with the importance of managing your blood sugar levels. However, when diabetes is accompanied by renal complications, a new dimension of care arises. The kidneys, the remarkable filtration system of our bodies, play a crucial role in maintaining overall health. They filter waste products, regulate fluid balance, and help control blood pressure. But when kidney function is compromised, as often seen in diabetic kidney disease, a unique set of challenges emerges.

The Diabetic Renal Diet recognizes the intricate connection between diabetes and kidney health. It aims to strike a delicate balance between controlling blood sugar levels and providing optimal nutrition for kidney function. By embracing this diet, you not only manage your diabetes effectively but also slow down the progression of kidney disease and protect the longevity of your kidneys.

## IMPORTANCE OF NUTRIENT CONTROL AND PORTION MANAGEMENT: BUILDING A SOLID FOUNDATION

To understand the Diabetic Renal Diet, let us delve into its core principles, starting with nutrient control. Scientific studies have shown that individuals with diabetes and kidney disease benefit from specific nutrient adjustments that promote kidney health and stabilize blood sugar levels. A key focus is on managing protein intake, as excessive protein can place strain on the kidneys. The diet emphasizes high-quality, plant-based proteins, such as legumes, tofu, and tempeh, while moderating the consumption of animal-based proteins.

In addition to protein, careful attention is given to sodium, potassium, and phosphorus. Sodium control helps manage fluid balance and blood pressure, while potassium and phosphorus regulation prevent electrolyte imbalances and minimize the workload on the kidneys. Incorporating a variety of fresh fruits and vegetables, whole grains, and lean proteins allows for a balanced intake of these essential nutrients.

Portion management is another fundamental aspect of the Diabetic Renal Diet. It is crucial to be mindful of portion sizes to avoid overloading the kidneys and straining blood sugar control. Measuring and monitoring food quantities, using tools such as portion control plates or food scales, can help you achieve this balance. By embracing portion management, you can savor the flavors you love while keeping your diabetes and kidney health in check.

## EMBRACING EMOTIONAL TRANSFORMATION: NURTURING YOUR WELL-BEING

The Diabetic Renal Diet is not merely a list of dos and don'ts; it is a transformative journey that encompasses both physical and emotional well-being. As you embark on this path, it is vital to recognize the emotional aspects of managing diabetes and kidney disease. Feelings of frustration, fear, and overwhelm may arise, but it is important to remember that you are not alone.

Seeking support from healthcare professionals, such as registered dietitians or diabetes educators, can be invaluable in navigating this emotional terrain. They can provide personalized guidance, practical tips, and emotional support, helping you embrace the challenges with resilience and determination. Connecting with support groups or online communities of individuals facing similar journeys can also provide a sense of camaraderie and a safe space to share experiences.

Remember, this journey is not about deprivation or restriction; it is about empowerment and self-care. It is about embracing the opportunity to nurture your health, both physically and emotionally. The Diabetic Renal Diet invites you to embark on this path with an open heart and a determination to cultivate balance and wellness in your life.

# CHAPTER 3: ESSENTIAL NUTRIENTS FOR DIABETIC RENAL DIETS

In the world of diabetic renal diets, understanding and managing essential nutrients play a crucial role in promoting overall health and well-being. This chapter explores the impact of carbohydrates, protein, sodium, potassium, fluid balance, as well as the management of phosphorus and calcium. By delving into the scientific underpinnings and practical applications of these nutrients, we aim to empower you to make informed choices that will not only support your diabetic renal diet but also nurture your emotional well-being.

## CARBOHYDRATES AND BLOOD SUGAR CONTROL:

Carbohydrates are the primary source of energy for our bodies. However, for individuals with diabetes, the relationship between carbohydrates and blood sugar control is a delicate balance. When consumed, carbohydrates are broken down into glucose, leading to an increase in blood sugar levels. Therefore, it is essential to choose the right types and quantities of carbohydrates to maintain stable blood sugar levels.

Fiber-rich carbohydrates such as whole grains, legumes, and vegetables are excellent choices for diabetic renal diets. These foods provide essential nutrients while promoting satiety and supporting digestive health. By slowing down the digestion and absorption of glucose, they help regulate blood sugar levels and prevent sudden spikes or drops. Examples of fiber-rich carbohydrates include brown rice, quinoa, lentils, and leafy greens.

## PROTEIN AND KIDNEY FUNCTION:

Protein is the building block of life, playing a crucial role in cell growth, repair, and maintenance. However, for individuals with renal complications, protein intake requires careful consideration. The kidneys play a vital role in filtering waste products from the blood, and impaired kidney function can lead to the accumulation of toxins. Consequently, a restricted protein intake is often recommended to alleviate the burden on the kidneys.

When following a diabetic renal diet, it is important to choose high-quality protein sources that are low in saturated fats and phosphorus. Lean meats, such as skinless poultry, fish, and tofu, are excellent options. They provide essential amino acids while minimizing the strain on the kidneys. Additionally, plant-based protein sources like beans, lentils, and quinoa are rich in fiber, promoting satiety and aiding in blood sugar control.

## SODIUM, POTASSIUM, AND FLUID BALANCE:

Sodium and potassium are electrolytes that play crucial roles in maintaining fluid balance, nerve function, and muscle contractions. However, in the context of diabetic renal diets, careful management of these electrolytes is necessary to support kidney health.

Sodium intake should be limited to prevent fluid retention and high blood pressure, which can strain the kidneys. Processed foods, canned goods, and salty snacks are often high in sodium and should be avoided or consumed in moderation. Instead, flavor your meals with herbs, spices, and natural seasonings to enhance taste without adding unnecessary sodium.

On the other hand, potassium is essential for normal cell function, but elevated potassium levels can be harmful to individuals with compromised kidney function. It is important to balance potassium intake by choosing low-potassium options such as apples, berries, cabbage, and green beans, while limiting high-potassium foods like bananas, oranges, tomatoes, and potatoes. Striking this balance promotes healthy kidney function and supports overall well-being.

Fluid balance is another critical aspect of diabetic renal diets. Individuals with renal complications may experience fluid retention, requiring careful monitoring of fluid intake. It is essential to follow the guidance of your healthcare provider regarding fluid restrictions and to make mindful choices to prevent dehydration or overload.

## PHOSPHORUS AND CALCIUM MANAGEMENT:

Phosphorus and calcium are essential minerals that work in harmony to support bone health, nerve function, and muscle contractions. However, individuals with renal complications often experience imbalances in these minerals, necessitating specific attention to their management.

High levels of phosphorus in the blood can lead to bone disease and cardiovascular complications. Therefore, it is crucial to limit phosphorus intake by avoiding or minimizing phosphorus-rich foods such as processed meats, carbonated beverages, and dairy products. Instead, choose lower phosphorus alternatives such as fresh fruits, vegetables, and lean protein sources.

Calcium plays a vital role in maintaining bone strength and preventing osteoporosis. However, due to the intricate relationship between phosphorus and calcium, managing calcium intake becomes equally important. While dairy products are traditionally associated with calcium, they can also be high in phosphorus. Explore alternative calcium sources like leafy greens (such as kale and collard greens), fortified non-dairy milk, and calcium-rich fish (such as salmon and sardines) to maintain optimal calcium levels.

## EMBRACING THE JOURNEY:

As we navigate the intricacies of essential nutrients for diabetic renal diets, it is important to remember that food is not only nourishment for the body but also a source of comfort and joy for the soul. While the scientific principles guide us in making informed choices, it is equally vital to approach our dietary journey with compassion and emotional well-being in mind.

Take pleasure in exploring new flavors, textures, and culinary experiences that align with your dietary needs. Engage your senses and savor the aromas, colors, and tastes that each meal brings. Embrace the power of mindful eating, cultivating a deeper connection with your food and its impact on your overall well-being.

Remember, you are embarking on a journey of self-care and self-discovery, nurturing your body and soul through the foods you choose. Let this chapter be a guide and a reminder that you have the power to make choices that support your health, promote balance, and bring joy to your life. Embrace the dance of nutrients, the symphony of flavors, and the nourishment that comes from nourishing both your body and soul.

# CHAPTER 4: MEAL PLANNING FOR DIABETES AND RENAL DISEASE

## CREATING A BALANCED PLATE

Meal planning plays a crucial role in managing both diabetes and renal disease. It involves selecting appropriate foods and considering their impact on blood sugar levels, sodium, potassium, phosphorus, calcium, and sugar intake. By creating a balanced plate, individuals with diabetes and renal disease can better control their blood sugar and maintain kidney health.

To create a balanced plate, it is important to include a variety of nutrient-dense foods while controlling portion sizes. Aim to fill half of your plate with non-starchy vegetables such as leafy greens, broccoli, cauliflower, and bell peppers. These vegetables are low in carbohydrates and calories, and they provide essential vitamins, minerals, and fiber.

The other half of your plate should be divided between lean protein sources and whole grains. Opt for lean protein options such as skinless chicken, turkey, fish, tofu, or legumes. These protein sources are important for building and repairing tissues, managing blood sugar levels, and supporting overall health. Whole grains such as brown rice, quinoa, whole wheat bread, or whole grain pasta provide fiber, which aids in digestion and helps control blood sugar levels.

## GLYCEMIC INDEX AND BLOOD SUGAR IMPACT

The glycemic index (GI) is a tool that measures how quickly carbohydrates in foods raise blood sugar levels. Foods with a high GI are digested and absorbed rapidly, causing a rapid increase in blood sugar levels. On the other hand, foods with a low GI are digested and absorbed more slowly, resulting in a gradual and more controlled rise in blood sugar levels.

For individuals with diabetes and renal disease, it is beneficial to focus on consuming foods with a low or moderate GI to prevent spikes in blood sugar. Some examples of low GI foods include non-starchy vegetables, whole grains, legumes, and certain fruits such as berries and apples. It is important to note that GI should not be the sole determinant of food choices, as portion sizes and overall meal composition also play a crucial role.

## RECOMMENDED DAILY INTAKE OF SODIUM, POTASSIUM, PHOSPHORUS, CALCIUM, AND SUGAR IN DIABETIC RENAL PATIENTS

Managing sodium, potassium, phosphorus, calcium, and sugar intake is essential for individuals with diabetes and renal disease. Here are the recommended daily intake guidelines for these nutrients:

- Sodium: Limiting sodium intake is crucial for managing blood pressure and preventing fluid retention. The American Heart Association recommends limiting sodium intake to **less than 2,300 milligrams per day** for most adults. However, for individuals with hypertension or kidney disease, the recommendation is often lower, typically around **1,500 milligrams per day.**

- Potassium: Potassium is an essential mineral that helps regulate fluid balance, nerve function, and muscle contractions. However, for individuals with renal disease, excessive potassium intake can be harmful. The recommended daily intake of potassium for most adults is around **2,600-3,400 milligrams per day.** However, for those with kidney disease, you should aim for lower keeping your daily intake between **2,500-3000 milligrams per day**. More importantly, individualized recommendations from a healthcare professional are crucial to avoid potassium imbalances.

- Phosphorus: High levels of phosphorus in the blood can be detrimental to kidney health. It is important to limit phosphorus intake by avoiding processed foods, sodas, and foods high in phosphorus additives. The recommended daily intake of phosphorus for individuals with renal disease is typically around **800-1,200 milligrams per day**, but it may vary depending on the stage of kidney disease and individual needs.

- Calcium: Calcium is vital for maintaining bone health and muscle function. The recommended daily intake of calcium for most adults is around **1,000-1,200 milligrams per day**. However, individuals with renal disease may need to adjust their calcium intake based on their specific needs and any accompanying conditions.

- Sugar: Monitoring sugar intake is important for managing blood sugar levels in individuals with diabetes. The American Diabetes Association recommends limiting added sugar intake to no more than 10% of total daily calories. Personally, I would recommend reducing your sugar intake to a maximum of **6 teaspoons per day or less. It is equivalent to 25 grams of sugar daily**. It is essential to focus on consuming whole foods and minimizing processed foods and sugary beverages.

## SAMPLE MEAL PLANS FOR DIFFERENT CALORIC NEEDS

Creating personalized meal plans based on individual caloric needs is important for individuals with diabetes and renal disease. Here are some sample meal plans:

### 1500-CALORIE MEAL PLAN:

- Breakfast: Veggie omelette with egg whites, spinach, mushrooms, and tomatoes + whole wheat toast
- Snack: Greek yogurt with berries
- Lunch: Grilled chicken breast with steamed broccoli and quinoa
- Snack: Carrot sticks with hummus
- Dinner: Baked salmon with roasted asparagus and brown rice
- Dessert: Sugar-free jello with whipped cream

### 1800-CALORIE MEAL PLAN:

- Breakfast: Overnight oats with almond milk, chia seeds, and mixed berries
- Snack: Handful of unsalted almonds

- Lunch: Turkey wrap with whole wheat tortilla, lean turkey, lettuce, and tomatoes + side salad
- Snack: Apple slices with peanut butter
- Dinner: Baked cod with lemon and herbs, served with steamed green beans and sweet potato
- Dessert: Baked apple with cinnamon and a sprinkle of granola

## 2000-CALORIE MEAL PLAN:

- Breakfast: Vegetable scramble with eggs, bell peppers, onions, and a sprinkle of low-fat cheese + whole grain toast
- Snack: Greek yogurt with sliced banana
- Lunch: Quinoa salad with grilled chicken, mixed vegetables, and a lemon vinaigrette
- Snack: Celery sticks with almond butter
- Dinner: Lean beef stir-fry with a variety of colorful vegetables and brown rice
- Dessert: Sugar-free yogurt parfait with layers of berries and crushed nuts

Remember, these sample meal plans are for reference purposes only. It is crucial to consult with a registered dietitian or healthcare professional to tailor a meal plan that meets your specific needs and considers any individual dietary restrictions or preferences.

By focusing on a balanced plate, considering the glycemic index, managing sodium, potassium, phosphorus, calcium, and sugar intake, and customizing meal plans based on individual caloric needs, individuals with diabetes and renal disease can take proactive steps towards optimizing their health and well-being.

# CHAPTER 5: SMART SHOPPING FOR DIABETIC RENAL DIETS

## READING FOOD LABELS AND MAKING INFORMED CHOICES

When following a diabetic renal diet, making smart choices at the grocery store is crucial for managing both diabetes and renal health. In this chapter, we will explore the art of reading food labels and provide you with invaluable tips to help you make informed choices while shopping. By understanding the information on food labels and being aware of key nutrients, you can better control your blood sugar levels and maintain optimal renal function.

Food labels are your gateway to understanding the nutritional composition of packaged foods. Let's dive into the essential components of a food label:

- Serving Size: Pay close attention to the serving size mentioned on the label. This information allows you to accurately assess the nutrients you consume.
- Total Carbohydrates: Carbohydrates have the most significant impact on blood sugar levels. Be mindful of the total carbohydrate content and the specific types of carbohydrates present, such as sugars, fiber, and starches.
- Added Sugars: Excessive sugar consumption can lead to spikes in blood sugar levels and negatively impact kidney function. Keep an eye out for added sugars in the ingredient list and aim to choose foods with minimal added sugars.

- Fiber: Fiber plays a crucial role in regulating blood sugar levels and promoting optimal digestion. Look for foods that are rich in dietary fiber to support a healthy diabetic renal diet.

- Sodium: Individuals with diabetes and renal conditions often need to limit their sodium intake. High sodium levels can lead to increased blood pressure and strain on the kidneys. Select foods with lower sodium content or opt for reduced-sodium alternatives.

- Protein: Protein is essential for building and repairing body tissues. However, individuals with kidney disease may require controlled protein intake. Look for foods that provide high-quality, low-phosphorus protein sources such as lean meats, poultry, fish, tofu, and legumes.

- Phosphorus and Potassium: For those with renal issues, monitoring phosphorus and potassium intake is crucial. Excessive phosphorus can lead to bone and heart problems, while high potassium levels can disrupt heart rhythm. Choose foods with lower phosphorus and potassium levels and limit the intake of processed and packaged foods, which are often high in these minerals.

## GROCERY SHOPPING TIPS FOR DIABETES AND RENAL HEALTH

Now that we understand how to read food labels effectively, let's explore some practical tips to make your grocery shopping experience both efficient and health-conscious:

- Plan Ahead: Create a weekly meal plan and make a shopping list accordingly. Planning your meals in advance not only helps you stay organized but also ensures that you choose diabetic renal-friendly foods.

- Shop the Perimeter: The outer aisles of the grocery store typically contain fresh produce, lean meats, and dairy products. Focus on filling your cart with nutrient-dense whole foods from these sections.

- Fresh Produce: Load up on a variety of colorful fruits and vegetables. These natural sources of vitamins, minerals, and fiber are essential for maintaining overall health and managing diabetes and renal conditions.

- Lean Protein Sources: Opt for lean cuts of meat, such as skinless chicken breast, turkey, and fish. These protein sources are lower in saturated fat and phosphorus, making them ideal choices for a diabetic renal diet.

- Whole Grains: Choose whole grain options like whole wheat bread, brown rice, quinoa, and oats. These provide essential nutrients and fiber while promoting better blood sugar control.

- Low-Fat Dairy Alternatives: If you have kidney disease, consider lower-potassium alternatives like almond milk or soy milk. Select low-fat or fat-free options to limit saturated fat and phosphorus intake.

- Canned Goods: When purchasing canned goods, opt for low-sodium or no-added-salt varieties. Rinse canned beans and vegetables under water to reduce their sodium content further.

- Snack Smart: Look for snacks that are low in added sugars and sodium. Choose options like unsalted nuts, fresh fruits, or homemade trail mix to satisfy your cravings without compromising your health.

## BUILDING A DIABETIC RENAL-FRIENDLY PANTRY

To make meal preparation easier and more convenient, it's essential to stock your pantry with diabetic renal-friendly staples. Here are some key items to include:

- Grains and Legumes: Whole wheat flour, brown rice, quinoa, lentils, and low-sodium canned beans are versatile ingredients that can form the base of many diabetic renal-friendly meals.
- Herbs and Spices: Flavor your dishes with herbs and spices instead of excessive salt. Dried herbs like basil, oregano, and thyme, as well as spices such as cinnamon, turmeric, and ginger, add depth and complexity to your cooking.
- Cooking Oils: Opt for heart-healthy oils such as olive oil, avocado oil, or canola oil. These provide healthier fat options and can be used for sautéing or dressing salads.
- Low-Sodium Broth and Stocks: Use low-sodium vegetable or chicken broth as a flavorful base for soups, stews, and sauces. These options add depth to your dishes without contributing excessive sodium.
- Nut Butters: Look for unsalted nut butters like almond butter or peanut butter. They serve as a nutritious spread or ingredient in recipes while providing healthy fats and protein.

- Canned Tomatoes: Stock up on canned tomatoes, which can be used as a base for sauces, soups, and stews. Choose low-sodium varieties to minimize your sodium intake.
- Nuts and Seeds: Almonds, walnuts, chia seeds, and flaxseeds are excellent sources of healthy fats, fiber, and protein. Keep them on hand for snacking or as toppings for salads and yogurt.

By building a well-stocked pantry, you can easily prepare diabetic renal-friendly meals at home, minimizing the need for processed or unhealthy options.

# CHAPTER 6: COOKING TECHNIQUES AND TIPS FOR DIABETIC RENAL DIETS

## HEALTHY COOKING METHODS FOR KIDNEY-FRIENDLY MEALS

When it comes to managing diabetes and renal health, adopting a kidney-friendly diet is crucial. In this chapter, we will explore cooking techniques and tips specifically tailored for individuals following a diabetic renal diet. These techniques will not only support your blood sugar control but also promote optimal kidney function and overall health.

The kidneys play a vital role in filtering waste products from the bloodstream, regulating fluid balance, and maintaining electrolyte levels. For individuals with both diabetes and renal complications, it is essential to follow a diet that is low in sodium, phosphorus, and potassium while still providing adequate nutrition. The right cooking methods and strategies can significantly contribute to achieving these goals.

One of the primary considerations when cooking for a diabetic renal diet is choosing healthy cooking methods that minimize the addition of excessive fats or salts. Let's explore some of the best cooking techniques for kidney-friendly meals:

- Grilling: Grilling is a fantastic method for preparing kidney-friendly meals. It allows you to add smoky flavors to your food without the need for excessive oils or salts. Grilling meats, fish, and vegetables not only enhances their natural flavors but also helps to reduce the need for added sodium. Scientific data suggests that grilling can help retain the nutritional integrity of food. Research shows that grilling lean meats such as chicken or fish can help preserve their protein content and reduce the formation of harmful compounds, such as advanced glycation end products (AGEs), which are linked to inflammation and oxidative stress. By opting for lean cuts of meat and marinating them with kidney-friendly herbs and spices, you can create flavorful and healthy grilled dishes.

- Steaming: Steaming is a gentle and kidney-friendly cooking method that helps retain the natural flavors, textures, and nutrients of the ingredients. Steaming vegetables, fish, and poultry requires minimal added fats, making it an ideal choice for individuals following a diabetic renal diet. Studies have shown that steaming vegetables helps preserve their water-soluble vitamins, such as vitamin C and B vitamins, which are essential for overall health and wellbeing. Moreover, steaming is a great way to cook vegetables like broccoli, cauliflower, and asparagus, which are rich in fiber, low in potassium, and beneficial for individuals with kidney disease.

- Roasting: Roasting is another versatile cooking technique that can be adapted to suit a diabetic renal diet. By using a hot oven, you can achieve caramelization and enhance the natural sweetness of vegetables, fruits, and meats without adding excessive fats or sodium. Research indicates that roasting vegetables can increase their antioxidant content, which is beneficial for individuals with diabetes and kidney disease. Vegetables like bell peppers, onions, and carrots can be roasted to create delicious and kidney-friendly side dishes.

## REDUCING SODIUM AND ENHANCING FLAVORS

Reducing sodium intake is crucial for individuals with diabetes and kidney disease, as excessive sodium can contribute to fluid retention and increased blood pressure. However, it's important to note that reducing sodium doesn't mean sacrificing flavor. By incorporating the right herbs, spices, and cooking techniques, you can create delicious and kidney-friendly meals without relying on excess salt.

- Flavorful Herbs and Spices: Herbs and spices are excellent alternatives to sodium when it comes to adding flavor to your dishes. For example, using herbs like basil, oregano, thyme, and rosemary can elevate the taste of your meals without increasing sodium levels. Spices such as turmeric, cumin, paprika, and cinnamon can also add depth and complexity to your recipes.
- Citrus Juices and Vinegars: Citrus juices, such as lemon or lime juice, and vinegars like apple cider vinegar or balsamic vinegar, can add tanginess and brightness to your dishes. They can be used as marinades, dressings, or finishing touches to enhance flavors without relying on excess sodium.
- Low-Sodium Broths and Stocks: When cooking soups, stews, or sauces, opt for low-sodium broths or stocks as a base. These alternatives provide flavor without the added sodium found in traditional broths or stocks. You can also

make your own broths by simmering vegetables and herbs to extract their natural flavors.

## MEAL PREPARATION AND BATCH COOKING

Meal preparation and batch cooking can be game-changers for individuals following a diabetic renal diet. By dedicating a specific time for meal planning and cooking, you can ensure that you have kidney-friendly meals readily available throughout the week. This approach not only saves time but also helps you maintain control over your diet and portion sizes.

Here are some tips for successful meal preparation and batch cooking:

- Plan Your Meals: Take time to plan your meals for the week, considering your dietary restrictions, nutritional needs, and personal preferences. Create a shopping list based on your meal plan to ensure you have all the necessary ingredients on hand.
- Cook in Bulk: When cooking, prepare larger portions than you need for one meal. This allows you to portion and store the leftovers for future consumption. Invest in quality storage containers that are suitable for freezing or refrigerating meals.
- Label and Date: Properly label and date your stored meals to ensure freshness and easy identification. Include reheating instructions if necessary.
- Variety and Versatility: Prepare a variety of dishes that can be repurposed throughout the week. For example, grilled chicken breasts can be used in

salads, sandwiches, or wraps. Roasted vegetables can be added to omelets, stir-fries, or grain bowls. This approach ensures that you have a range of kidney-friendly options at your disposal.

By following these cooking techniques, reducing sodium, and embracing meal preparation and batch cooking, you can create delicious, kidney-friendly meals that support your diabetes management and promote optimal renal health. With a little creativity and the right strategies, you can enjoy a diverse and flavorful diet while taking control of your health journey. Remember, every meal is an opportunity to nourish your body and indulge in the pleasures of food while maintaining your overall wellbeing.

# CHAPTER 7: BREAKFASTS TO START THE DAY RIGHT

## VEGETABLE EGG SCRAMBLE WITH SPINACH AND MUSHROOMS

Time: 15 minutes

Servings: 2

Ingredients:

- 4 large eggs
- 1 cup spinach, chopped
- 1 cup mushrooms, sliced
- 1/4 teaspoon salt substitute
- 1/4 teaspoon black pepper
- 1 teaspoon olive oil

Directions:

- Heat olive oil in a non-stick skillet over medium heat.
- Add mushrooms and sauté until softened, about 3-4 minutes.
- Add spinach and cook until wilted, about 2 minutes.
- In a bowl, whisk the eggs with salt substitute and black pepper.
- Pour the egg mixture over the vegetables in the skillet.
- Stir gently until the eggs are fully cooked and scrambled, about 3-4 minutes.
- Remove from heat and serve hot.

Nutritional Information per serving:

- Calories: 160
- Protein: 15g
- Fat: 10g
- Carbohydrates: 4g
- Fiber: 1g
- Sodium: 120mg
- Potassium: 250mg
- Phosphorus: 120mg

## OATMEAL WITH FRESH BERRIES AND CINNAMON

Time: 10 minutes

Servings: 1

Ingredients:

- 1/2 cup rolled oats
- 1 cup water
- 1/4 cup fresh berries (such as blueberries, raspberries, or strawberries)
- 1/2 teaspoon cinnamon
- 1 tablespoon chopped nuts (such as almonds or walnuts)

Directions:

- In a small saucepan, bring the water to a boil.
- Add the rolled oats and reduce heat to low.
- Cook, stirring occasionally, for about 5 minutes until the oats are tender and creamy.
- Remove from heat and transfer to a bowl.
- Top with fresh berries, sprinkle with cinnamon, and garnish with chopped nuts.
- Serve warm.

Nutritional Information per serving:

- Calories: 200
- Protein: 6g
- Fat: 6g
- Carbohydrates: 32g
- Fiber: 6g
- Sodium: 0mg
- Potassium: 150mg
- Phosphorus: 120mg

## GREEK YOGURT PARFAIT WITH LOW-SUGAR GRANOLA AND CHOPPED NUTS

Time: 5 minutes

Servings: 1

Ingredients:

- 1/2 cup low-fat Greek yogurt
- 1/4 cup low-sugar granola
- 1 tablespoon chopped nuts (such as almonds or pistachios)
- 1/4 cup fresh berries (such as strawberries or blueberries)

Directions:

- In a glass or bowl, layer half of the Greek yogurt.
- Sprinkle half of the low-sugar granola over the yogurt.
- Add half of the chopped nuts on top.
- Repeat the layers with the remaining yogurt, granola, and nuts.
- Finish by topping with fresh berries.
- Serve chilled.

Nutritional Information per serving:

- Calories: 250
- Protein: 18g
- Fat: 10g
- Carbohydrates: 25g
- Fiber: 4g
- Sodium: 80mg
- Potassium: 200mg
- Phosphorus: 150mg

## WHOLE WHEAT PANCAKES WITH SUGAR-FREE FRUIT COMPOTE

Time: 20 minutes

Servings: 2

Ingredients:

- 1 cup whole wheat flour
- 1 tablespoon baking powder
- 1/4 teaspoon salt substitute
- 1 tablespoon stevia (or your preferred sugar substitute)
- 1 cup almond milk (unsweetened)
- 1 large egg
- 1 teaspoon vanilla extract
- Cooking spray

*For the Sugar-Free Fruit Compote:*

- 1 cup mixed berries (such as blueberries, raspberries, and strawberries)
- 1 tablespoon lemon juice
- 1/2 teaspoon stevia (or your preferred sugar substitute)

Directions:

- In a large bowl, whisk together the whole wheat flour, baking powder, salt substitute, and stevia.
- In a separate bowl, whisk together almond milk, egg, and vanilla extract.
- Pour the wet ingredients into the dry ingredients and stir until just combined.
- Heat a non-stick skillet or griddle over medium heat and coat with cooking spray.
- Pour 1/4 cup of batter onto the skillet for each pancake.
- Cook until bubbles form on the surface, then flip and cook for another 1-2 minutes until golden brown.
- For the sugar-free fruit compote, combine the mixed berries, lemon juice, and stevia in a small saucepan.
- Cook over medium heat, stirring occasionally, until the berries soften and release their juices, about 5-7 minutes.
- Serve the pancakes topped with the sugar-free fruit compote.

Nutritional Information per serving (including fruit compote):

- Calories: 270
- Protein: 10g
- Fat: 6g
- Carbohydrates: 48g
- Fiber: 9g
- Sodium: 220mg
- Potassium: 300mg
- Phosphorus: 220mg

## QUINOA BREAKFAST BOWL WITH ALMOND MILK AND SLICED ALMONDS

Time: 15 minutes

Servings: 2

Ingredients:

- 1 cup cooked quinoa
- 1 cup unsweetened almond milk
- 1/2 teaspoon cinnamon
- 1 tablespoon chopped nuts (such as almonds or walnuts)
- 1 tablespoon unsweetened coconut flakes
- 1/4 cup fresh berries (such as blueberries or raspberries)
- 1 teaspoon honey (optional)

Directions:

- In a saucepan, heat the cooked quinoa and almond milk over medium heat.
- Stir in the cinnamon and cook for about 5 minutes until warmed through.
- Divide the quinoa mixture into serving bowls.
- Top with chopped nuts, coconut flakes, fresh berries, and drizzle with honey if desired.
- Serve warm.

Nutritional Information per serving:

- Calories: 220
- Protein: 8g
- Fat: 8g
- Carbohydrates: 31g
- Fiber: 6g
- Sodium: 80mg
- Potassium: 200mg
- Phosphorus: 150mg

## EGG WHITE OMELETTE WITH LOW-POTASSIUM VEGETABLES

Time: 15 minutes

Servings: 1

Ingredients:

- 3 egg whites
- 1/4 cup chopped low-potassium vegetables (such as bell peppers, zucchini, and onions)
- 1/4 teaspoon salt substitute
- 1/4 teaspoon black pepper
- 1 teaspoon olive oil

Directions:

- In a bowl, whisk the egg whites with salt substitute and black pepper.
- Heat olive oil in a non-stick skillet over medium heat.
- Add the chopped vegetables and sauté until softened, about 3-4 minutes.
- Pour the egg whites over the vegetables and cook until the omelette is set, about 3-4 minutes.
- Carefully fold the omelette in half and transfer it to a plate.
- Serve hot.

Nutritional Information per serving:

- Calories: 90
- Protein: 15g
- Fat: 2g
- Carbohydrates: 2g
- Fiber: 0g
- Sodium: 200mg
- Potassium: 150mg
- Phosphorus: 70mg

## CHIA SEED PUDDING WITH UNSWEETENED COCONUT FLAKES

Time: 5 minutes (plus chilling time)

Servings: 2

Ingredients:

- 1/4 cup chia seeds
- 1 cup unsweetened almond milk

- 1/4 teaspoon vanilla extract
- 1 tablespoon unsweetened coconut flakes
- Fresh berries for topping

Directions:

- In a bowl, combine the chia seeds, almond milk, and vanilla extract.
- Whisk well to avoid clumps.
- Cover the bowl and refrigerate for at least 2 hours or overnight until the mixture thickens.
- Stir the pudding before serving to distribute the chia seeds evenly.
- Divide the pudding into serving bowls.
- Top with unsweetened coconut flakes and fresh berries.
- Serve chilled.

Nutritional Information per serving:

- Calories: 120
- Protein: 5g
- Fat: 7g
- Carbohydrates: 10g
- Fiber: 8g
- Sodium: 80mg
- Potassium: 150mg
- Phosphorus: 120mg

## COTTAGE CHEESE WITH SLICED PEACHES AND FLAXSEED

Time: 5 minutes

Servings: 1

Ingredients:

- 1/2 cup low-fat cottage cheese
- 1/2 peach, sliced
- 1 tablespoon ground flaxseed
- 1/2 teaspoon honey (optional)

Directions:

- In a bowl, spoon the low-fat cottage cheese.
- Top with sliced peaches and sprinkle with ground flaxseed.

- Drizzle with honey if desired.
- Serve chilled.

Nutritional Information per serving:

- Calories: 150
- Protein: 14g
- Fat: 5g
- Carbohydrates: 14g
- Fiber: 3g
- Sodium: 250mg
- Potassium: 220mg
- Phosphorus: 220mg

## AVOCADO AND TOMATO TOAST ON WHOLE GRAIN BREAD

Time: 10 minutes

Servings: 1

Ingredients:

- 1 slice of whole grain bread, toasted
- 1/4 avocado, mashed
- 1 small tomato, sliced
- 1/4 teaspoon salt substitute
- 1/4 teaspoon black pepper
- Fresh basil leaves for garnish

Directions:

- Spread the mashed avocado evenly on the toasted bread slice.
- Top with sliced tomatoes.
- Sprinkle with salt substitute and black pepper.
- Garnish with fresh basil leaves.
- Serve immediately.

Nutritional Information per serving:

- Calories: 160
- Protein: 5g
- Fat: 8g
- Carbohydrates: 20g
- Fiber: 6g
- Sodium: 250mg
- Potassium: 350mg
- Phosphorus: 120mg

## BUCKWHEAT PANCAKES WITH SUGAR-FREE MAPLE SYRUP

Time: 20 minutes

Servings: 2

Ingredients:

- 1/2 cup buckwheat flour
- 1/2 cup whole wheat flour
- 1 tablespoon baking powder
- 1/4 teaspoon salt substitute
- 1 tablespoon stevia (or your preferred sugar substitute)
- 1 cup almond milk (unsweetened)
- 1 large egg
- Cooking spray
- Sugar-free maple syrup for serving

Directions:

- In a large bowl, whisk together the buckwheat flour, whole wheat flour, baking powder, salt substitute, and stevia.
- In a separate bowl, whisk together almond milk and egg.
- Pour the wet ingredients into the dry ingredients and stir until just combined.
- Heat a non-stick skillet or griddle over medium heat and coat with cooking spray.
- Pour 1/4 cup of batter onto the skillet for each pancake.
- Cook until bubbles form on the surface, then flip and cook for another 1-2 minutes until golden brown.
- Serve the pancakes with sugar-free maple syrup.

Nutritional Information per serving (including maple syrup):

- Calories: 240
- Protein: 9g
- Fat: 4g
- Carbohydrates: 45g

- Fiber: 6g
- Sodium: 240mg
- Potassium: 320mg
- Phosphorus: 220mg

## VEGGIE BREAKFAST BURRITO WITH WHOLE WHEAT TORTILLA

Time: 15 minutes

Servings: 1

Ingredients:

- 1 whole wheat tortilla
- 2 egg whites
- 1/4 cup chopped low-potassium vegetables (such as bell peppers, zucchini, and onions)
- 2 tablespoons low-sodium salsa
- 2 tablespoons low-sodium shredded cheese
- 1/4 avocado, sliced
- Salt substitute and black pepper to taste

Directions:

- Heat the whole wheat tortilla according to package instructions.
- In a non-stick skillet, cook the egg whites over medium heat until set.
- Remove the cooked egg whites from the skillet and set aside.
- In the same skillet, sauté the chopped vegetables until tender.
- Spread the low-sodium salsa on the warmed tortilla.
- Layer the cooked egg whites, sautéed vegetables, low-sodium shredded cheese, and sliced avocado.
- Season with salt substitute and black pepper.
- Roll up the tortilla, folding in the sides, to form a burrito.
- Serve warm.

Nutritional Information per serving:

- Calories: 290
- Protein: 17g
- Fat: 12g
- Carbohydrates: 32g
- Fiber: 9g
- Sodium: 230mg
- Potassium: 400mg
- Phosphorus: 250mg

## SMOOTHIE BOWL WITH SPINACH, ALMOND MILK, AND BERRIES

Time: 10 minutes

Servings: 1

Ingredients:

- 1 cup fresh spinach
- 1/2 cup unsweetened almond milk
- 1/2 banana, frozen
- 1/2 cup frozen berries (such as blueberries or raspberries)
- 1 tablespoon chia seeds
- Fresh berries and sliced almonds for topping

Directions:

- In a blender, combine the fresh spinach, almond milk, frozen banana, frozen berries, and chia seeds.
- Blend until smooth and creamy.
- Pour the smoothie into a bowl.
- Top with fresh berries and sliced almonds.
- Serve immediately.

Nutritional Information per serving:

- Calories: 180
- Protein: 6g
- Fat: 8g
- Carbohydrates: 24g
- Fiber: 9g
- Sodium: 130mg
- Potassium: 480mg
- Phosphorus: 200mg

## LOW-SODIUM BREAKFAST CASSEROLE WITH TURKEY SAUSAGE AND BELL PEPPERS

Time: 45 minutes

Servings: 4

Ingredients:

- 4 turkey sausage links, cooked and sliced
- 1 red bell pepper, diced
- 1 green bell pepper, diced
- 1 small onion, diced
- 4 large eggs
- 1/2 cup low-fat milk
- 1/4 teaspoon salt substitute
- 1/4 teaspoon black pepper
- 1/4 teaspoon dried thyme
- Cooking spray

Directions:

- Preheat the oven to 350°F (175°C).
- In a non-stick skillet, cook the turkey sausage links until browned and fully cooked.
- Slice the cooked sausages into bite-sized pieces and set aside.
- In the same skillet, sauté the diced bell peppers and onion until softened.
- In a bowl, whisk together the eggs, low-fat milk, salt substitute, black pepper, and dried thyme.
- Spray a baking dish with cooking spray.
- Spread the sautéed bell peppers and onion in an even layer in the baking dish.
- Top with the cooked turkey sausage pieces.
- Pour the egg mixture over the vegetables and sausage.
- Bake in the preheated oven for about 30 minutes or until the eggs are set and the top is golden brown.

- Remove from the oven and let cool slightly before serving.

Nutritional Information per serving:

- Calories: 220
- Protein: 18g
- Fat: 10g
- Carbohydrates: 12g
- Fiber: 2g
- Sodium: 220mg
- Potassium: 350mg
- Phosphorus: 280mg

## ALMOND FLOUR BANANA MUFFINS WITH STEVIA

Time: 30 minutes

Servings: 12 muffins

Ingredients:

- 2 cups almond flour
- 1 teaspoon baking powder
- 1/2 teaspoon baking soda
- 1/4 teaspoon salt substitute
- 2 ripe bananas, mashed
- 1/4 cup melted coconut oil
- 1/4 cup stevia (or your preferred sugar substitute)
- 3 large eggs
- 1 teaspoon vanilla extract

Directions:

- Preheat the oven to 350°F (175°C) and line a muffin tin with paper liners.
- In a bowl, whisk together the almond flour, baking powder, baking soda, and salt substitute.
- In a separate bowl, mix the mashed bananas, melted coconut oil, stevia, eggs, and vanilla extract until well combined.
- Pour the wet ingredients into the dry ingredients and stir until just combined.
- Divide the batter evenly among the prepared muffin cups, filling each about 3/4 full.

- Bake in the preheated oven for 18-20 minutes or until a toothpick inserted into the center of a muffin comes out clean.
- Remove from the oven and let cool in the pan for 5 minutes, then transfer to a wire rack to cool completely.

Nutritional Information per serving (1 muffin):

- Calories: 180
- Protein: 6g
- Fat: 15g
- Carbohydrates: 7g
- Fiber: 3g
- Sodium: 100mg
- Potassium: 200mg
- Phosphorus: 110mg

## SWEET POTATO HASH BROWNS WITH LOW-SODIUM SEASONING

Time: 30 minutes

Servings: 4

Ingredients:

- 2 medium sweet potatoes, peeled and grated
- 1/2 small onion, grated
- 1/4 teaspoon salt substitute
- 1/4 teaspoon black pepper
- 1/4 teaspoon garlic powder
- 1/4 teaspoon paprika
- Cooking spray

Directions:

- Place the grated sweet potatoes and grated onion in a clean kitchen towel or cheesecloth.
- Squeeze out any excess moisture from the sweet potatoes and onion.
- Transfer the dry sweet potatoes and onion to a bowl.
- Add the salt substitute, black pepper, garlic powder, and

paprika to the sweet potatoes and onion.
- Mix well to combine all the ingredients.
- Heat a non-stick skillet over medium heat and coat with cooking spray.
- Scoop about 1/4 cup of the sweet potato mixture onto the skillet and flatten with a spatula to form a hash brown patty.
- Cook for 3-4 minutes on each side until golden brown and crispy.
- Repeat with the remaining sweet potato mixture.
- Serve hot.

Nutritional Information per serving:

- Calories: 90
- Protein: 2g
- Fat: 0g
- Carbohydrates: 21g
- Fiber: 3g
- Sodium: 120mg
- Potassium: 310mg
- Phosphorus: 45mg

## RICOTTA AND BERRY STUFFED FRENCH TOAST WITH WHOLE GRAIN BREAD

Time: 20 minutes

Servings: 2

Ingredients:

- 4 slices whole grain bread
- 1/2 cup low-fat ricotta cheese
- 1/2 teaspoon vanilla extract
- 1/2 cup fresh berries (such as strawberries or blueberries)
- 2 large eggs
- 1/4 cup unsweetened almond milk
- Cooking spray

Directions:

- In a bowl, mix the low-fat ricotta cheese and vanilla extract until well combined.
- Spread the ricotta mixture on two slices of bread.
- Top with fresh berries and cover with the remaining two slices of bread to form sandwiches.
- In a shallow dish, whisk together the eggs and almond milk.
- Heat a non-stick skillet over medium heat and coat with cooking spray.
- Dip each sandwich into the egg mixture, turning to coat both sides.
- Place the dipped sandwiches in the skillet and cook for 2-3 minutes on each side until golden brown and crispy.
- Remove from the skillet and let cool slightly before serving.

Nutritional Information per serving:

- Calories: 320
- Protein: 17g
- Fat: 10g
- Carbohydrates: 40g
- Fiber: 8g
- Sodium: 380mg
- Potassium: 350mg
- Phosphorus: 240mg

## VEGGIE FRITTATA WITH ZUCCHINI, BELL PEPPERS, AND ONION

Time: 30 minutes

Servings: 4

Ingredients:

- 1 tablespoon olive oil
- 1 small zucchini, sliced
- 1/2 red bell pepper, diced
- 1/2 green bell pepper, diced
- 1 small onion, diced
- 4 large eggs
- 1/4 cup low-fat milk
- 1/4 teaspoon salt substitute

- 1/4 teaspoon black pepper
- 1/4 teaspoon dried oregano
- Cooking spray

Directions:

- Preheat the oven to 350°F (175°C).
- Heat olive oil in a non-stick skillet over medium heat.
- Add the zucchini, red bell pepper, green bell pepper, and onion. Sauté until the vegetables are tender.
- In a bowl, whisk together the eggs, low-fat milk, salt substitute, black pepper, and dried oregano.
- Coat a round baking dish with cooking spray.
- Transfer the sautéed vegetables to the baking dish.
- Pour the egg mixture over the vegetables.
- Bake in the preheated oven for 20-25 minutes or until the frittata is set and lightly golden.
- Remove from the oven and let cool slightly before serving.

Nutritional Information per serving:

- Calories: 150
- Protein: 9g
- Fat: 8g
- Carbohydrates: 10g
- Fiber: 2g
- Sodium: 190mg
- Potassium: 380mg
- Phosphorus: 140mg

## BREAKFAST QUINOA WITH SLICED APPLES AND CINNAMON

Time: 20 minutes

Servings: 2

Ingredients:

- 1/2 cup quinoa, rinsed
- 1 cup water
- 1 small apple, sliced
- 1/2 teaspoon cinnamon
- 1 tablespoon chopped walnuts
- 1 tablespoon honey (optional)

Directions:

- In a saucepan, combine the quinoa and water. Bring to a boil, then reduce heat to low and simmer for 15 minutes or until the quinoa is tender and the water is absorbed.
- Remove from heat and let sit for 5 minutes.
- Fluff the quinoa with a fork.
- Divide the cooked quinoa into two bowls.
- Top with sliced apples, cinnamon, chopped walnuts, and drizzle with honey if desired.
- Serve warm.

Nutritional Information per serving:

- Calories: 200
- Protein: 5g
- Fat: 6g
- Carbohydrates: 35g
- Fiber: 5g
- Sodium: 5mg
- Potassium: 270mg
- Phosphorus: 140mg

## LOW-SUGAR BRAN MUFFINS WITH WALNUTS

Time: 40 minutes

Servings: 12 muffins

Ingredients:

- 1 1/2 cups wheat bran
- 1 cup unsweetened almond milk
- 1/4 cup unsweetened applesauce
- 1/4 cup vegetable oil
- 1/4 cup stevia (or your preferred sugar substitute)
- 1 teaspoon vanilla extract
- 1 cup whole wheat flour

- 1 teaspoon baking powder
- 1/2 teaspoon baking soda
- 1/4 teaspoon salt substitute
- 1/4 cup chopped walnuts

Directions:

- Preheat the oven to 375°F (190°C) and line a muffin tin with paper liners.
- In a bowl, combine the wheat bran and almond milk. Let sit for 5 minutes to soften the bran.
- Stir in the applesauce, vegetable oil, stevia, and vanilla extract until well combined.
- In a separate bowl, whisk together the whole wheat flour, baking powder, baking soda, and salt substitute.
- Add the dry ingredients to the wet ingredients and stir until just combined.
- Fold in the chopped walnuts.
- Divide the batter evenly among the prepared muffin cups, filling each about 2/3 full.
- Bake in the preheated oven for 18-20 minutes or until a toothpick inserted into the center of a muffin comes out clean.
- Remove from the oven and let cool in the pan for 5 minutes, then transfer to a wire rack to cool completely.

Nutritional Information per serving (1 muffin):

- Calories: 110
- Protein: 4g
- Fat: 5g
- Carbohydrates: 17g
- Fiber: 5g
- Sodium: 70mg
- Potassium: 180mg
- Phosphorus: 100mg

## VEGGIE BREAKFAST WRAP WITH EGG WHITES AND LOW-SODIUM CHEESE

Time: 15 minutes

Servings: 1

Ingredients:

- 1 large whole wheat tortilla
- 3 large egg whites
- 1/4 cup diced low-potassium vegetables (such as bell peppers, tomatoes, and onions)
- 1 slice low-sodium cheese
- Salt substitute and black pepper to taste

Directions:

- Heat the whole wheat tortilla according to package instructions.
- In a non-stick skillet, cook the egg whites over medium heat until set.
- Remove the cooked egg whites from the skillet and set aside.
- In the same skillet, sauté the diced vegetables until tender.
- Place the cooked egg whites on the warmed tortilla.
- Top with sautéed vegetables and place the low-sodium cheese slice on top.
- Season with salt substitute and black pepper.
- Roll up the tortilla, folding in the sides, to form a wrap.
- Serve warm.

Nutritional Information per serving:

- Calories: 200
- Protein: 20g
- Fat: 7g
- Carbohydrates: 18g
- Fiber: 3g
- Sodium: 210mg
- Potassium: 270mg
- Phosphorus: 200mg

# CHAPTER 8: SATISFYING SOUPS AND SALADS

## TOMATO AND BASIL SOUP WITH LOW-SODIUM BROTH

Time: 30 minutes

Servings: 4

Ingredients:

- 1 tablespoon olive oil
- 1 onion, diced
- 2 cloves garlic, minced
- 4 cups low-sodium vegetable broth
- 4 large tomatoes, diced
- 1/4 cup fresh basil leaves, chopped
- Salt and pepper to taste

Directions:

- Heat olive oil in a large pot over medium heat.
- Add diced onion and minced garlic, sauté until translucent.
- Add low-sodium vegetable broth and diced tomatoes to the pot. Bring to a boil, then reduce heat and simmer for 15 minutes.
- Stir in chopped basil leaves and season with salt and pepper.
- Use an immersion blender or transfer the soup to a blender to puree until smooth.
- Serve hot with a sprinkle of fresh basil leaves.

Nutritional Information (per serving):

- Calories: 120
- Fat: 4g
- Carbohydrates: 18g
- Protein: 3g

- Sodium: 150mg
- Potassium: 500mg
- Phosphorus: 70mg

## CUCUMBER AND AVOCADO SALAD WITH LEMON VINAIGRETTE

Time: 15 minutes

Servings: 4

Ingredients:

- 2 cucumbers, sliced
- 1 avocado, diced
- 1/4 red onion, thinly sliced
- Juice of 1 lemon
- 1 tablespoon extra-virgin olive oil
- 1 teaspoon honey or sugar substitute
- Salt and pepper to taste

Directions:

- In a large bowl, combine sliced cucumbers, diced avocado, and thinly sliced red onion.
- In a separate small bowl, whisk together lemon juice, olive oil, honey (or sugar substitute), salt, and pepper to make the vinaigrette.
- Drizzle the vinaigrette over the cucumber and avocado mixture.
- Gently toss to coat the salad evenly.
- Serve chilled.

Nutritional Information (per serving):

- Calories: 120
- Fat: 9g
- Carbohydrates: 10g
- Protein: 2g
- Sodium: 10mg
- Potassium: 400mg
- Phosphorus: 60mg

## LENTIL SOUP WITH CARROTS AND CELERY

Time: 1 hour 15 minutes

Servings: 6

Ingredients:

- 1 cup dried lentils, rinsed
- 2 carrots, diced
- 2 stalks celery, diced
- 1 onion, diced
- 2 cloves garlic, minced
- 4 cups low-sodium vegetable broth
- 1 bay leaf
- 1 teaspoon dried thyme
- Salt and pepper to taste

Directions:

- In a large pot, combine rinsed lentils, diced carrots, diced celery, diced onion, minced garlic, low-sodium vegetable broth, bay leaf, dried thyme, salt, and pepper.
- Bring the mixture to a boil, then reduce heat and simmer for 1 hour or until lentils are tender.
- Remove the bay leaf and season with additional salt and pepper if needed.
- Serve hot.

Nutritional Information (per serving):

- Calories: 180
- Fat: 0.5g
- Carbohydrates: 34g
- Protein: 12g
- Sodium: 100mg
- Potassium: 420mg
- Phosphorus: 160mg

## GREEK SALAD WITH FETA CHEESE AND OLIVES (LOW-SODIUM VERSION)

Time: 15 minutes

Servings: 4

Ingredients:

- 4 cups mixed salad greens
- 1 cucumber, diced
- 1 bell pepper, diced
- 1/4 red onion, thinly sliced
- 1 cup cherry tomatoes, halved
- 1/4 cup Kalamata olives, pitted and sliced
- 2 ounces reduced-fat feta cheese, crumbled
- Juice of 1 lemon
- 2 tablespoons extra-virgin olive oil
- 1 teaspoon dried oregano
- Salt and pepper to taste

Directions:

- In a large salad bowl, combine mixed salad greens, diced cucumber, diced bell pepper, thinly sliced red onion, cherry tomatoes, Kalamata olives, and crumbled feta cheese.
- In a small bowl, whisk together lemon juice, extra-virgin olive oil, dried oregano, salt, and pepper to make the dressing.
- Drizzle the dressing over the salad.
- Gently toss to combine all the ingredients.
- Serve chilled.

Nutritional Information (per serving):

- Calories: 150
- Fat: 10g
- Carbohydrates: 12g
- Protein: 6g
- Sodium: 180mg
- Potassium: 400mg
- Phosphorus: 120mg

## CHICKEN AND VEGETABLE SOUP WITH HERBS AND SPICES

Time: 45 minutes

Servings: 6

Ingredients:

- 1 tablespoon olive oil
- 1 onion, diced
- 2 carrots, diced
- 2 stalks celery, diced
- 2 cloves garlic, minced
- 1 pound boneless, skinless chicken breasts, diced
- 6 cups low-sodium chicken broth
- 1 bay leaf
- 1 teaspoon dried thyme
- 1 teaspoon dried rosemary
- Salt and pepper to taste

Directions:

- In a large pot, heat olive oil over medium heat.
- Add diced onion, diced carrots, diced celery, and minced garlic. Sauté until vegetables are tender.
- Add diced chicken breasts, low-sodium chicken broth, bay leaf, dried thyme, dried rosemary, salt, and pepper to the pot.
- Bring the mixture to a boil, then reduce heat and simmer for 30 minutes or until chicken is cooked through.
- Remove the bay leaf and season with additional salt and pepper if needed.
- Serve hot.

Nutritional Information (per serving):

- Calories: 180
- Fat: 4g
- Carbohydrates: 6g
- Protein: 25g
- Sodium: 100mg
- Potassium: 400mg
- Phosphorus: 220mg

## SPINACH SALAD WITH STRAWBERRIES AND BALSAMIC DRESSING (LOW-SUGAR VERSION)

Time: 10 minutes

Servings: 4

Ingredients:

- 4 cups baby spinach leaves
- 1 cup strawberries, sliced
- 1/4 cup chopped walnuts
- 2 tablespoons crumbled goat cheese
- 2 tablespoons balsamic vinegar
- 1 tablespoon extra-virgin olive oil
- 1 teaspoon honey or sugar substitute
- Salt and pepper to taste

Directions:

- In a large salad bowl, combine baby spinach leaves, sliced strawberries, chopped walnuts, and crumbled goat cheese.
- In a small bowl, whisk together balsamic vinegar, extra-virgin olive oil, honey (or sugar substitute), salt, and pepper to make the dressing.
- Drizzle the dressing over the salad.
- Gently toss to coat the salad evenly.
- Serve chilled.

Nutritional Information (per serving):

- Calories: 140
- Fat: 10g
- Carbohydrates: 9g
- Protein: 4g
- Sodium: 80mg
- Potassium: 350mg
- Phosphorus: 70mg

## BEAN AND VEGETABLE MINESTRONE SOUP (LOW-SODIUM VERSION)

Time: 1 hour

Servings: 6

Ingredients:

- 1 tablespoon olive oil
- 1 onion, diced
- 2 carrots, diced
- 2 stalks celery, diced
- 2 cloves garlic, minced
- 1 zucchini, diced
- 1 yellow squash, diced
- 1 can (15 ounces) low-sodium diced tomatoes
- 4 cups low-sodium vegetable broth
- 1 can (15 ounces) kidney beans, rinsed and drained
- 1 can (15 ounces) cannellini beans, rinsed and drained
- 1 teaspoon dried oregano
- 1 teaspoon dried basil
- Salt and pepper to taste

Directions:

- In a large pot, heat olive oil over medium heat.
- Add diced onion, diced carrots, diced celery, minced garlic, diced zucchini, and diced yellow squash. Sauté until vegetables are tender.
- Add low-sodium diced tomatoes, low-sodium vegetable broth, kidney beans, cannellini beans, dried oregano, dried basil, salt, and pepper to the pot.
- Bring the mixture to a boil, then reduce heat and simmer for 45 minutes.
- Season with additional salt and pepper if needed.
- Serve hot.

Nutritional Information (per serving):

- Calories: 220

- Fat: 3g
- Carbohydrates: 40g
- Protein: 10g
- Sodium: 150mg
- Potassium: 800mg
- Phosphorus: 180mg

## QUINOA SALAD WITH ROASTED VEGETABLES AND LEMON DRESSING

Time: 45 minutes

Servings: 4

Ingredients:

- 1 cup quinoa
- 2 cups low-sodium vegetable broth
- 1 small eggplant, diced
- 1 red bell pepper, diced
- 1 yellow bell pepper, diced
- 1 zucchini, diced
- 1 tablespoon olive oil
- Juice of 1 lemon
- 2 tablespoons chopped fresh parsley
- Salt and pepper to taste

Directions:

- Preheat the oven to 400°F (200°C).
- In a saucepan, combine quinoa and low-sodium vegetable broth. Bring to a boil, then reduce heat, cover, and simmer for 15 minutes or until quinoa is tender and liquid is absorbed.
- While the quinoa is cooking, spread diced eggplant, diced red bell pepper, diced yellow bell pepper, and diced zucchini on a baking sheet. Drizzle with olive oil, salt, and pepper.
- Roast the vegetables in the preheated oven for 20-25 minutes or until tender and slightly caramelized.
- In a small bowl, whisk together lemon juice, chopped fresh

parsley, salt, and pepper to make the dressing.

- In a large mixing bowl, combine cooked quinoa, roasted vegetables, and the lemon dressing. Toss to combine all the ingredients.
- Serve warm or chilled.

Nutritional Information (per serving):

- Calories: 240
- Fat: 6g
- Carbohydrates: 39g
- Protein: 8g
- Sodium: 100mg
- Potassium: 600mg
- Phosphorus: 160mg

## BROCCOLI AND CHEDDAR SOUP WITH LOW-SODIUM STOCK

Time: 30 minutes

Servings: 4

Ingredients:

- 1 tablespoon olive oil
- 1 onion, diced
- 2 cloves garlic, minced
- 4 cups low-sodium vegetable broth
- 4 cups broccoli florets
- 1 cup shredded low-sodium cheddar cheese
- Salt and pepper to taste

Directions:

- In a large pot, heat olive oil over medium heat.
- Add diced onion and minced garlic, sauté until translucent.
- Add low-sodium vegetable broth and broccoli florets to the pot. Bring to a boil, then reduce heat and simmer for 15 minutes or until the broccoli is tender.

- Use an immersion blender or transfer the soup to a blender to puree until smooth.
- Return the soup to the pot and stir in shredded low-sodium cheddar cheese until melted and well combined.
- Season with salt and pepper to taste.
- Serve hot.

Nutritional Information (per serving):

- Calories: 200
- Fat: 10g
- Carbohydrates: 18g
- Protein: 12g
- Sodium: 150mg
- Potassium: 600mg
- Phosphorus: 220mg

## MIXED GREEN SALAD WITH GRILLED CHICKEN AND LOW-PHOSPHORUS DRESSING

Time: 30 minutes

Servings: 4

Ingredients:

- 4 cups mixed salad greens
- 1 grilled chicken breast, sliced
- 1/4 cup cherry tomatoes, halved
- 1/4 cup sliced cucumber
- 1/4 cup sliced radishes
- 2 tablespoons chopped fresh parsley
- 2 tablespoons low-phosphorus salad dressing (look for one specifically labeled as low-phosphorus)
- Salt and pepper to taste

Directions:

- In a large salad bowl, combine mixed salad greens, sliced grilled chicken breast, cherry tomatoes, sliced cucumber, sliced radishes, and chopped fresh parsley.
- Drizzle the low-phosphorus salad dressing over the salad.

- Gently toss to coat the salad evenly.
- Season with salt and pepper to taste.
- Serve chilled.

Nutritional Information (per serving):

- Calories: 180
- Fat: 4g
- Carbohydrates: 6g
- Protein: 30g
- Sodium: 120mg
- Potassium: 450mg
- Phosphorus: 150mg

## BUTTERNUT SQUASH SOUP WITH CINNAMON AND NUTMEG

Time: 1 hour

Servings: 6

Ingredients:

- 1 butternut squash, peeled, seeded, and diced
- 1 onion, diced
- 2 carrots, diced
- 2 cloves garlic, minced
- 4 cups low-sodium vegetable broth
- 1 teaspoon ground cinnamon
- 1/2 teaspoon ground nutmeg
- Salt and pepper to taste

Directions:

- In a large pot, combine diced butternut squash, diced onion, diced carrots, minced garlic, low-sodium vegetable broth, ground cinnamon, ground nutmeg, salt, and pepper.
- Bring the mixture to a boil, then reduce heat and simmer for 30-40 minutes or until the vegetables are tender.
- Use an immersion blender or transfer the soup to a blender to puree until smooth.

- Return the soup to the pot and heat over low heat until warmed through.
- Season with additional salt and pepper if needed.
- Serve hot.

Nutritional Information (per serving):

- Calories: 150
- Fat: 1g
- Carbohydrates: 35g
- Protein: 3g
- Sodium: 100mg
- Potassium: 850mg
- Phosphorus: 100mg

## ASIAN CHICKEN SALAD WITH GINGER-SESAME DRESSING (LOW-SODIUM VERSION)

Time: 20 minutes

Servings: 4

Ingredients:

- 2 cups shredded cooked chicken breast
- 4 cups shredded Napa cabbage
- 1 cup shredded carrots
- 1/2 cup sliced scallions
- 1/4 cup chopped fresh cilantro
- 2 tablespoons low-sodium soy sauce
- 1 tablespoon rice vinegar
- 1 tablespoon sesame oil
- 1 teaspoon grated fresh ginger
- 1 clove garlic, minced
- 1/4 teaspoon red pepper flakes (optional)
- Salt and pepper to taste

Directions:

- In a large salad bowl, combine shredded cooked chicken breast, shredded Napa cabbage, shredded carrots, sliced scallions, and chopped fresh cilantro.
- In a small bowl, whisk together low-sodium soy sauce, rice

vinegar, sesame oil, grated fresh ginger, minced garlic, red pepper flakes (optional), salt, and pepper to make the dressing.

- Drizzle the dressing over the salad.
- Gently toss to coat the salad evenly.
- Serve chilled.

Nutritional Information (per serving):

- Calories: 200
- Fat: 6g
- Carbohydrates: 10g
- Protein: 25g
- Sodium: 200mg
- Potassium: 550mg
- Phosphorus: 200mg

## CAULIFLOWER AND LEEK SOUP WITH LOW-SODIUM SEASONING

Time: 40 minutes

Servings: 4

Ingredients:

- 1 head cauliflower, chopped into florets
- 2 leeks, white and light green parts only, sliced
- 2 cloves garlic, minced
- 4 cups low-sodium vegetable broth
- 1 teaspoon dried thyme
- 1/2 teaspoon ground turmeric
- Salt and pepper to taste

Directions:

- In a large pot, combine cauliflower florets, sliced leeks, minced garlic, low-sodium vegetable broth, dried thyme, ground turmeric, salt, and pepper.
- Bring the mixture to a boil, then reduce heat and simmer for 20-

25 minutes or until the cauliflower is tender.

- Use an immersion blender or transfer the soup to a blender to puree until smooth.
- Return the soup to the pot and heat over low heat until warmed through.
- Season with additional salt and pepper if needed.
- Serve hot.

Nutritional Information (per serving):

- Calories: 100
- Fat: 1g
- Carbohydrates: 20g
- Protein: 5g
- Sodium: 150mg
- Potassium: 900mg
- Phosphorus: 100mg

## WATERMELON AND FETA SALAD WITH MINT (LOW-SODIUM VERSION)

Time: 15 minutes

Servings: 4

Ingredients:

- 4 cups cubed watermelon
- 1/2 cup crumbled low-sodium feta cheese
- 1/4 cup chopped fresh mint leaves
- 1 tablespoon balsamic vinegar
- 1 tablespoon extra-virgin olive oil
- Salt and pepper to taste

Directions:

- In a large salad bowl, combine cubed watermelon, crumbled low-sodium feta cheese, and chopped fresh mint leaves.
- In a small bowl, whisk together balsamic vinegar, extra-virgin

olive oil, salt, and pepper to make the dressing.

- Drizzle the dressing over the salad.
- Gently toss to coat the salad evenly.
- Serve chilled.

Nutritional Information (per serving):

- Calories: 90
- Fat: 4g
- Carbohydrates: 10g
- Protein: 3g
- Sodium: 200mg
- Potassium: 250mg
- Phosphorus: 70mg

## NAVY BEAN AND VEGETABLE SOUP (LOW-SODIUM VERSION)

Time: 1 hour 30 minutes

Servings: 6

Ingredients:

- 1 tablespoon olive oil
- 1 onion, diced
- 2 carrots, diced
- 2 stalks celery, diced
- 2 cloves garlic, minced
- 2 cups diced butternut squash
- 1 can (15 ounces) navy beans, rinsed and drained
- 4 cups low-sodium vegetable broth
- 1 teaspoon dried thyme
- 1 teaspoon dried rosemary
- Salt and pepper to taste

Directions:

- In a large pot, heat olive oil over medium heat.
- Add diced onion, diced carrots, diced celery, and minced garlic. Sauté until vegetables are tender.
- Add diced butternut squash, navy beans, low-sodium vegetable broth, dried thyme, dried

rosemary, salt, and pepper to the pot.

- Bring the mixture to a boil, then reduce heat and simmer for 1 hour or until the vegetables are tender and the flavors are well combined.
- Season with additional salt and pepper if needed.
- Serve hot.

Nutritional Information (per serving):

- Calories: 180
- Fat: 2g
- Carbohydrates: 33g
- Protein: 10g
- Sodium: 200mg
- Potassium: 700mg
- Phosphorus: 150mg

## CAPRESE SALAD WITH FRESH MOZZARELLA AND BALSAMIC GLAZE (LOW-SODIUM VERSION)

Time: 10 minutes

Servings: 4

Ingredients:

- 2 large tomatoes, sliced
- 8 ounces fresh mozzarella cheese, sliced
- 1/4 cup fresh basil leaves
- 1 tablespoon balsamic glaze (look for one specifically labeled as low-sodium)
- Salt and pepper to taste

Directions:

- On a serving platter, alternate slices of tomatoes and fresh mozzarella cheese.
- Top with fresh basil leaves.
- Drizzle the balsamic glaze over the salad.
- Season with salt and pepper to taste.

- Serve at room temperature.

Nutritional Information (per serving):

- Calories: 180
- Fat: 12g
- Carbohydrates: 6g
- Protein: 12g
- Sodium: 100mg
- Potassium: 400mg
- Phosphorus: 200mg

## ROASTED RED PEPPER AND TOMATO SOUP (LOW-SODIUM VERSION)

Time: 1 hour 30 minutes

Servings: 6

Ingredients:

- 3 red bell peppers
- 4 large tomatoes
- 1 onion, diced
- 2 cloves garlic, minced
- 4 cups low-sodium vegetable broth
- 2 tablespoons tomato paste
- 1 teaspoon dried basil
- 1/2 teaspoon dried oregano
- Salt and pepper to taste

Directions:

- Preheat the oven to 400°F (200°C).
- Place whole red bell peppers and tomatoes on a baking sheet. Roast in the preheated oven for 30-40 minutes or until the skins are charred and blistered.
- Remove the roasted vegetables from the oven and let them cool slightly. Peel off the skins, remove the seeds, and chop the flesh.
- In a large pot, heat olive oil over medium heat.
- Add diced onion and minced garlic. Sauté until translucent.
- Add chopped roasted red bell peppers, chopped roasted tomatoes, low-sodium vegetable broth, tomato paste, dried basil, dried oregano, salt, and pepper to the pot.
- Bring the mixture to a boil, then reduce heat and simmer for 30-40 minutes to allow the flavors to meld together.

- Use an immersion blender or transfer the soup to a blender to puree until smooth.
- Return the soup to the pot and heat over low heat until warmed through.
- Season with additional salt and pepper if needed.
- Serve hot.

Nutritional Information (per serving):

- Calories: 120
- Fat: 1g
- Carbohydrates: 24g
- Protein: 4g
- Sodium: 150mg
- Potassium: 750mg
- Phosphorus: 80mg

## QUINOA AND BLACK BEAN SALAD WITH LIME-CILANTRO DRESSING (LOW-SODIUM VERSION)

Time: 30 minutes

Servings: 4

Ingredients:

- 1 cup cooked quinoa
- 1 can (15 ounces) black beans, rinsed and drained
- 1 cup diced tomatoes
- 1/2 cup diced red onion
- 1/4 cup chopped fresh cilantro
- 2 tablespoons freshly squeezed lime juice
- 1 tablespoon extra-virgin olive oil
- 1 clove garlic, minced
- Salt and pepper to taste

Directions:

- In a large salad bowl, combine cooked quinoa, black beans, diced tomatoes, diced red onion, and chopped fresh cilantro.
- In a small bowl, whisk together freshly squeezed lime juice, extra-virgin olive oil, minced garlic, salt, and pepper to make the dressing.
- Drizzle the dressing over the salad.
- Gently toss to coat the salad evenly.
- Serve chilled.

Nutritional Information (per serving):

- Calories: 220

- Fat: 6g
- Carbohydrates: 34g
- Protein: 10g
- Sodium: 100mg
- Potassium: 500mg
- Phosphorus: 200mg

## CHICKEN NOODLE SOUP WITH WHOLE WHEAT NOODLES (LOW-SODIUM VERSION)

Time: 1 hour 30 minutes

Servings: 6

Ingredients:

- 1 tablespoon olive oil
- 1 onion, diced
- 2 carrots, diced
- 2 stalks celery, diced
- 2 cloves garlic, minced
- 4 cups low-sodium chicken broth
- 2 cups water
- 2 boneless, skinless chicken breasts, cooked and shredded
- 2 cups cooked whole wheat noodles
- 1 teaspoon dried thyme
- 1 bay leaf
- Salt and pepper to taste

Directions:

- In a large pot, heat olive oil over medium heat.
- Add diced onion, diced carrots, diced celery, and minced garlic. Sauté until vegetables are tender.
- Add low-sodium chicken broth, water, shredded cooked chicken breasts, cooked whole wheat noodles, dried thyme, bay leaf, salt, and pepper to the pot.
- Bring the mixture to a boil, then reduce heat and simmer for 1 hour to allow the flavors to meld together.
- Remove the bay leaf before serving.
- Season with additional salt and pepper if needed.
- Serve hot.

Nutritional Information (per serving):

- Calories: 220
- Fat: 5g
- Carbohydrates: 20g
- Protein: 25g
- Sodium: 150mg
- Potassium: 400mg
- Phosphorus: 200mg

## SPINACH AND STRAWBERRY SALAD WITH GOAT CHEESE AND WALNUTS (LOW-SODIUM VERSION)

Time: 15 minutes

Servings: 4

Ingredients:

- 4 cups baby spinach leaves
- 1 cup sliced strawberries
- 1/4 cup crumbled goat cheese
- 1/4 cup chopped walnuts
- 2 tablespoons balsamic vinegar
- 1 tablespoon extra-virgin olive oil
- Salt and pepper to taste

Directions:

- In a large salad bowl, combine baby spinach leaves, sliced strawberries, crumbled goat cheese, and chopped walnuts.
- In a small bowl, whisk together balsamic vinegar, extra-virgin olive oil, salt, and pepper to make the dressing.
- Drizzle the dressing over the salad.
- Gently toss to coat the salad evenly.
- Serve chilled.

Nutritional Information (per serving):

- Calories: 150
- Fat: 11g
- Carbohydrates: 9g
- Protein: 5g
- Sodium: 100mg
- Potassium: 300mg
- Phosphorus: 80mg

# CHAPTER 9: WHOLESOME MAIN DISHES

## BAKED SALMON WITH DILL AND LEMON

Time: 30 minutes

Servings: 4

Ingredients:

- 4 salmon fillets (4-6 ounces each)
- 1 tablespoon fresh dill, chopped
- 1 lemon, sliced
- 2 teaspoons olive oil
- Salt and pepper to taste

Directions:

- Preheat the oven to 375°F (190°C). Line a baking sheet with parchment paper.
- Place the salmon fillets on the prepared baking sheet.
- Drizzle the olive oil evenly over the salmon fillets.
- Sprinkle the chopped dill, salt, and pepper over the salmon.
- Place a couple of lemon slices on top of each salmon fillet.
- Bake in the preheated oven for 15-20 minutes or until the salmon is cooked through and flakes easily with a fork.
- Remove from the oven and serve hot.

Nutritional Information (per serving):

- Calories: 250
- Protein: 25g
- Fat: 14g
- Carbohydrates: 2g
- Fiber: 1g

- Sodium: 80mg
- Potassium: 400mg
- Phosphorus: 250mg

## GRILLED CHICKEN BREAST WITH HERBS AND SPICES

Time: 25 minutes

Servings: 4

Ingredients:

- 4 boneless, skinless chicken breasts (4-6 ounces each)
- 1 teaspoon dried oregano
- 1 teaspoon dried basil
- 1 teaspoon garlic powder
- 1 teaspoon onion powder
- 1/2 teaspoon paprika
- Salt and pepper to taste
- Cooking spray

Directions:

- Preheat the grill to medium-high heat.
- In a small bowl, mix together the dried oregano, dried basil, garlic powder, onion powder, paprika, salt, and pepper.
- Season both sides of the chicken breasts evenly with the herb and spice mixture.
- Lightly coat the grill grates with cooking spray to prevent sticking.
- Place the seasoned chicken breasts on the preheated grill and cook for 6-8 minutes per side, or until the internal temperature reaches 165°F (74°C).
- Remove from the grill and let the chicken rest for a few minutes before serving.

Nutritional Information (per serving):

- Calories: 180
- Protein: 32g
- Fat: 4g
- Carbohydrates: 2g

- Fiber: 1g
- Sodium: 100mg
- Potassium: 320mg
- Phosphorus: 230mg

## SHRIMP STIR-FRY WITH LOW-SODIUM SOY SAUCE AND VEGETABLES

Time: 20 minutes

Servings: 4

Ingredients:

- 1 pound shrimp, peeled and deveined
- 2 tablespoons low-sodium soy sauce
- 1 tablespoon olive oil
- 1 garlic clove, minced
- 1 teaspoon grated fresh ginger
- 2 cups mixed vegetables (broccoli, bell peppers, snap peas, carrots)
- Salt and pepper to taste

Directions:

- In a small bowl, combine the low-sodium soy sauce, minced garlic, and grated ginger. Set aside.
- Heat the olive oil in a large skillet or wok over medium-high heat.
- Add the shrimp to the skillet and stir-fry for 2-3 minutes until they turn pink and opaque. Remove the shrimp from the skillet and set aside.
- In the same skillet, add the mixed vegetables and stir-fry for 4-5 minutes until they are tender-crisp.
- Return the cooked shrimp to the skillet and pour the soy sauce mixture over the shrimp and vegetables.
- Stir-fry for an additional 1-2 minutes, ensuring the shrimp and vegetables are evenly coated with the sauce.

- Season with salt and pepper to taste.
- Serve hot.

Nutritional Information (per serving):

- Calories: 180
- Protein: 25g
- Fat: 5g
- Carbohydrates: 9g
- Fiber: 3g
- Sodium: 160mg
- Potassium: 320mg
- Phosphorus: 200mg

## TURKEY MEATBALLS WITH ZUCCHINI NOODLES AND TOMATO SAUCE

Time: 40 minutes

Servings: 4

Ingredients:

- 1 pound ground turkey
- 1/4 cup whole wheat breadcrumbs
- 1/4 cup grated Parmesan cheese
- 1/4 cup finely chopped onion
- 1 garlic clove, minced
- 1 tablespoon chopped fresh parsley
- 1 teaspoon dried oregano
- 1/2 teaspoon salt
- 1/4 teaspoon black pepper
- 2 large zucchini, spiralized into noodles
- 2 cups low-sodium tomato sauce
- Cooking spray

Directions:

- Preheat the oven to 375°F (190°C). Line a baking sheet with parchment paper and lightly coat it with cooking spray.
- In a large bowl, combine the ground turkey, breadcrumbs, Parmesan cheese, onion, garlic, parsley, oregano, salt, and pepper. Mix well until all

ingredients are evenly incorporated.

- Shape the turkey mixture into meatballs, approximately 1 inch in diameter, and place them on the prepared baking sheet.
- Bake the meatballs in the preheated oven for 20-25 minutes, or until cooked through and lightly browned.
- While the meatballs are baking, spray a large skillet with cooking spray and heat over medium heat.
- Add the zucchini noodles to the skillet and cook for 2-3 minutes, or until tender but still slightly crisp.
- Heat the low-sodium tomato sauce in a separate saucepan over medium heat.
- Once the meatballs are cooked, add them to the tomato sauce and simmer for a few minutes to allow the flavors to meld together.
- Serve the turkey meatballs with the zucchini noodles and tomato sauce.

Nutritional Information (per serving):

- Calories: 250
- Protein: 30g
- Fat: 9g
- Carbohydrates: 16g
- Fiber: 4g
- Sodium: 180mg
- Potassium: 700mg
- Phosphorus: 300mg

## BAKED COD WITH HERBED QUINOA PILAF

Time: 35 minutes

Servings: 4

Ingredients:

- 4 cod fillets (4-6 ounces each)
- 1 tablespoon lemon juice

- 1 teaspoon dried thyme
- 1 teaspoon dried parsley
- 1/2 teaspoon garlic powder
- 1/2 teaspoon onion powder
- Salt and pepper to taste
- 1 cup quinoa, rinsed
- 2 cups low-sodium vegetable broth
- 1/4 cup chopped fresh parsley (for garnish)

Directions:

- Preheat the oven to 400°F (200°C). Line a baking sheet with parchment paper.
- Place the cod fillets on the prepared baking sheet.
- Drizzle the lemon juice evenly over the cod fillets.
- In a small bowl, combine the dried thyme, dried parsley, garlic powder, onion powder, salt, and pepper. Sprinkle the herb mixture over the cod fillets.
- Bake in the preheated oven for 12-15 minutes, or until the cod is opaque and flakes easily with a fork.
- While the cod is baking, prepare the quinoa pilaf. In a medium saucepan, bring the vegetable broth to a boil.
- Add the rinsed quinoa to the boiling broth, reduce the heat to low, cover, and simmer for 15 minutes, or until the quinoa is cooked and the liquid is absorbed.
- Fluff the quinoa with a fork and stir in the chopped fresh parsley.
- Serve the baked cod over a bed of herbed quinoa pilaf.

Nutritional Information (per serving):

- Calories: 220
- Protein: 25g
- Fat: 2g
- Carbohydrates: 26g

- Fiber: 3g
- Sodium: 200mg
- Potassium: 600mg
- Phosphorus: 200mg

## GRILLED VEGETABLE SKEWERS WITH BALSAMIC GLAZE

Time: 30 minutes

Servings: 4

Ingredients:

- 2 zucchinis, sliced into rounds
- 1 red bell pepper, cut into chunks
- 1 yellow bell pepper, cut into chunks
- 1 red onion, cut into wedges
- 8 cherry tomatoes
- 2 tablespoons olive oil
- 2 tablespoons balsamic vinegar
- 1 tablespoon chopped fresh basil
- 1 tablespoon chopped fresh thyme
- Salt and pepper to taste

Directions:

- Preheat the grill to medium-high heat.
- Thread the zucchini rounds, bell pepper chunks, red onion wedges, and cherry tomatoes onto skewers, alternating the vegetables.
- In a small bowl, whisk together the olive oil, balsamic vinegar, chopped fresh basil, chopped fresh thyme, salt, and pepper.
- Brush the vegetable skewers with the balsamic glaze, making sure to coat them evenly.
- Place the vegetable skewers on the preheated grill and cook for 10-12 minutes, turning occasionally, until the vegetables are tender and lightly charred.
- Remove from the grill and serve hot.

Nutritional Information (per serving):

- Calories: 120
- Protein: 2g
- Fat: 7g
- Carbohydrates: 14g
- Fiber: 3g
- Sodium: 10mg
- Potassium: 450mg
- Phosphorus: 50mg

## BAKED TOFU WITH LOW-SODIUM TERIYAKI SAUCE AND BROWN RICE

Time: 45 minutes

Servings: 4

Ingredients:

- 1 block extra-firm tofu, pressed and drained
- 1/4 cup low-sodium teriyaki sauce
- 1 tablespoon low-sodium soy sauce
- 1 tablespoon honey or sugar substitute
- 1 tablespoon rice vinegar
- 1 tablespoon cornstarch
- 2 tablespoons water
- 2 cups cooked brown rice
- 2 green onions, thinly sliced (for garnish)
- Sesame seeds (for garnish)

Directions:

- Preheat the oven to 400°F (200°C). Line a baking sheet with parchment paper.
- Cut the pressed and drained tofu into cubes or slices.
- In a small bowl, whisk together the low-sodium teriyaki sauce, low-sodium soy sauce, honey or sugar substitute, and rice vinegar.
- Place the tofu on the prepared baking sheet and brush both sides

with the teriyaki sauce mixture, reserving some for serving.

- Bake in the preheated oven for 25-30 minutes, flipping the tofu halfway through, until the tofu is golden and crispy.
- In a small saucepan, whisk together the cornstarch and water until well combined.
- Place the saucepan over medium heat and cook, stirring constantly, until the mixture thickens and becomes translucent.
- Remove the saucepan from the heat and stir in the remaining teriyaki sauce mixture.
- Serve the baked tofu over a bed of cooked brown rice and drizzle with the teriyaki sauce. Garnish with sliced green onions and sesame seeds.

Nutritional Information (per serving):

- Calories: 280
- Protein: 12g
- Fat: 6g
- Carbohydrates: 47g
- Fiber: 4g
- Sodium: 200mg
- Potassium: 250mg
- Phosphorus: 150mg

## LEMON HERB GRILLED CHICKEN THIGHS WITH STEAMED BROCCOLI

Time: 35 minutes

Servings: 4

Ingredients:

- 4 chicken thighs, bone-in and skin-on
- Juice of 2 lemons
- Zest of 1 lemon
- 2 tablespoons chopped fresh parsley

- 1 tablespoon chopped fresh thyme
- 1 tablespoon olive oil
- Salt and pepper to taste
- 4 cups broccoli florets

Directions:

- Preheat the grill to medium heat.
- In a small bowl, whisk together the lemon juice, lemon zest, chopped fresh parsley, chopped fresh thyme, olive oil, salt, and pepper.
- Place the chicken thighs in a shallow dish and pour the lemon herb marinade over them. Make sure the chicken is coated evenly. Let it marinate for 15-20 minutes.
- Remove the chicken thighs from the marinade and grill them on the preheated grill for 12-15 minutes per side, or until the internal temperature reaches 165°F (74°C) and the chicken is fully cooked.
- While the chicken is grilling, steam the broccoli florets until they are tender-crisp. This typically takes about 5-7 minutes.
- Remove the chicken from the grill and let it rest for a few minutes before serving.
- Serve the grilled chicken thighs with steamed broccoli.

Nutritional Information (per serving):

- Calories: 320
- Protein: 28g
- Fat: 20g
- Carbohydrates: 10g
- Fiber: 4g
- Sodium: 160mg
- Potassium: 550mg
- Phosphorus: 200mg

## QUINOA-STUFFED BELL PEPPERS WITH GROUND TURKEY AND LOW-SODIUM SEASONING

Time: 50 minutes

Servings: 4

Ingredients:

- 4 bell peppers (any color), tops cut off and seeds removed
- 1/2 cup quinoa, rinsed
- 1 cup low-sodium chicken or vegetable broth
- 1/2 pound ground turkey
- 1/2 onion, finely chopped
- 1 garlic clove, minced
- 1/2 teaspoon dried oregano
- 1/2 teaspoon dried basil
- 1/2 teaspoon paprika
- 1/4 teaspoon salt
- 1/4 teaspoon black pepper
- 1/2 cup low-sodium tomato sauce

Directions:

- Preheat the oven to 375°F (190°C). Place the bell peppers in a baking dish.
- In a small saucepan, bring the chicken or vegetable broth to a boil. Add the rinsed quinoa, reduce the heat to low, cover, and simmer for 15 minutes, or until the quinoa is cooked and the liquid is absorbed.
- In a large skillet, cook the ground turkey over medium heat until browned and cooked through. Add the chopped onion and minced garlic and cook for an additional 2-3 minutes, until the onion is tender.
- Stir in the dried oregano, dried basil, paprika, salt, black pepper, and low-sodium tomato sauce. Cook for another 2-3 minutes to allow the flavors to meld together.

- Remove the skillet from the heat and stir in the cooked quinoa.
- Spoon the turkey-quinoa mixture into the bell peppers, filling them to the top.
- Place the filled bell peppers in the preheated oven and bake for 25-30 minutes, or until the peppers are tender and the filling is heated through.
- Remove from the oven and let them cool for a few minutes before serving.

Nutritional Information (per serving):

- Calories: 250
- Protein: 18g
- Fat: 8g
- Carbohydrates: 29g
- Fiber: 6g
- Sodium: 180mg
- Potassium: 500mg
- Phosphorus: 200mg

## EGGPLANT PARMESAN WITH WHOLE WHEAT PASTA (LOW-SODIUM VERSION)

Time: 1 hour 30 minutes

Servings: 4

Ingredients:

- 1 large eggplant, sliced into rounds
- 2 cups low-sodium tomato sauce
- 1/4 cup grated Parmesan cheese
- 1/4 cup whole wheat breadcrumbs
- 1/4 cup chopped fresh basil
- 2 tablespoons olive oil
- 2 cloves garlic, minced
- 8 ounces whole wheat pasta
- Salt and pepper to taste

Directions:

- Preheat the oven to 400°F (200°C). Line a baking sheet

- with parchment paper and brush it with olive oil.
- Place the eggplant slices on the prepared baking sheet. Brush the eggplant slices with olive oil and season with salt and pepper.
- Bake the eggplant slices in the preheated oven for 20-25 minutes, or until they are tender and lightly browned.
- In a medium saucepan, heat the low-sodium tomato sauce over medium heat.
- In a small bowl, combine the grated Parmesan cheese, whole wheat breadcrumbs, chopped fresh basil, minced garlic, salt, and pepper.
- Cook the whole wheat pasta according to the package instructions until al dente. Drain the pasta and set it aside.
- Remove the eggplant slices from the oven and reduce the oven temperature to 350°F (175°C).
- In a baking dish, spread a thin layer of the tomato sauce. Place a layer of baked eggplant slices on top of the sauce.
- Sprinkle a portion of the Parmesan breadcrumb mixture over the eggplant layer. Repeat the layers until all the eggplant slices and sauce are used, finishing with a layer of the Parmesan breadcrumb mixture on top.
- Bake the eggplant Parmesan in the preheated oven for 30-35 minutes, or until the top is golden and crispy.
- Serve the eggplant Parmesan with cooked whole wheat pasta.

Nutritional Information (per serving):

- Calories: 350
- Protein: 10g
- Fat: 10g
- Carbohydrates: 55g

- Fiber: 10g
- Sodium: 150mg
- Potassium: 600mg
- Phosphorus: 150mg

## BAKED CHICKEN WITH ROASTED BRUSSELS SPROUTS AND SWEET POTATOES

Time: 1 hour

Servings: 4

Ingredients:

- 4 chicken breasts, boneless and skinless
- 2 cups Brussels sprouts, halved
- 2 medium sweet potatoes, peeled and cut into cubes
- 2 tablespoons olive oil
- 1 teaspoon dried rosemary
- 1 teaspoon dried thyme
- 1/2 teaspoon garlic powder
- Salt and pepper to taste

Directions:

- Preheat the oven to 400°F (200°C). Line a baking sheet with parchment paper.
- In a large bowl, combine the Brussels sprouts, sweet potatoes, olive oil, dried rosemary, dried thyme, garlic powder, salt, and pepper. Toss to coat the vegetables evenly.
- Place the chicken breasts on the prepared baking sheet. Arrange the Brussels sprouts and sweet potatoes around the chicken.
- Bake in the preheated oven for 30-35 minutes, or until the chicken is cooked through and the vegetables are tender and golden brown.
- Remove from the oven and let it rest for a few minutes before serving.

Nutritional Information (per serving):

- Calories: 300
- Protein: 30g
- Fat: 8g
- Carbohydrates: 25g
- Fiber: 6g
- Sodium: 120mg
- Potassium: 800mg
- Phosphorus: 300mg

## GRILLED STEAK WITH MUSHROOM SAUCE AND STEAMED ASPARAGUS

Time: 40 minutes

Servings: 4

Ingredients:

- 4 steaks (such as sirloin or filet mignon), about 6 ounces each
- 2 cups sliced mushrooms
- 1/2 onion, thinly sliced
- 2 cloves garlic, minced
- 1 cup low-sodium beef broth
- 1/4 cup low-fat sour cream
- 1 tablespoon olive oil
- 1 teaspoon Worcestershire sauce
- 1 teaspoon Dijon mustard
- Salt and pepper to taste
- 1 pound asparagus, trimmed

Directions:

- Preheat the grill to medium-high heat.
- Season the steaks with salt and pepper on both sides.
- In a saucepan, heat the olive oil over medium heat. Add the sliced mushrooms, onion, and minced garlic. Cook until the mushrooms are tender and the onions are translucent.
- Add the low-sodium beef broth, Worcestershire sauce, and Dijon mustard to the saucepan. Bring the mixture to a boil and then reduce the heat to low. Simmer for 10 minutes.
- Remove the saucepan from the heat and stir in the low-fat sour

cream. Season with salt and pepper to taste. Keep warm.

- Grill the steaks on the preheated grill for about 4-5 minutes per side, or until they reach the desired level of doneness.
- While the steaks are grilling, steam the asparagus until tender-crisp, about 5-7 minutes.
- Remove the steaks from the grill and let them rest for a few minutes before serving.
- Serve the grilled steaks with the mushroom sauce and steamed asparagus.

Nutritional Information (per serving):

- Calories: 350
- Protein: 30g
- Fat: 18g
- Carbohydrates: 14g
- Fiber: 4g
- Sodium: 220mg
- Potassium: 800mg
- Phosphorus: 250mg

## LENTIL CURRY WITH BROWN RICE AND SPINACH

Time: 45 minutes

Servings: 4

Ingredients:

- 1 cup brown lentils, rinsed
- 1 onion, finely chopped
- 2 cloves garlic, minced
- 1 tablespoon grated fresh ginger
- 1 tablespoon curry powder
- 1/2 teaspoon ground cumin
- 1/2 teaspoon ground turmeric
- 1/4 teaspoon cayenne pepper (optional for spice)
- 2 cups low-sodium vegetable broth
- 1 can (14 ounces) diced tomatoes, undrained
- 2 cups packed fresh spinach leaves

- 1 cup cooked brown rice
- Salt to taste

Directions:

- In a large saucepan, heat a little water over medium heat. Add the chopped onion and cook until softened, about 5 minutes.
- Add the minced garlic and grated ginger to the saucepan. Cook for an additional 1-2 minutes.
- Stir in the curry powder, ground cumin, ground turmeric, and cayenne pepper (if using). Cook for another minute to toast the spices.
- Add the rinsed lentils, low-sodium vegetable broth, and diced tomatoes with their juice to the saucepan. Bring the mixture to a boil.
- Reduce the heat to low and simmer, covered, for 30-35 minutes, or until the lentils are tender and cooked through. Stir occasionally to prevent sticking.
- Stir in the fresh spinach leaves and cook for an additional 2-3 minutes, or until the spinach wilts.
- Season with salt to taste.
- Serve the lentil curry over cooked brown rice.

Nutritional Information (per serving):

- Calories: 320
- Protein: 18g
- Fat: 2g
- Carbohydrates: 60g
- Fiber: 14g
- Sodium: 150mg
- Potassium: 750mg
- Phosphorus: 300mg

## STIR-FRIED SHRIMP AND VEGETABLES WITH LOW-SODIUM SAUCE

Time: 25 minutes

Servings: 4

Ingredients:

- 1 pound shrimp, peeled and deveined
- 2 tablespoons low-sodium soy sauce
- 2 tablespoons rice vinegar
- 1 tablespoon cornstarch
- 1 tablespoon canola oil
- 1 onion, thinly sliced
- 2 cloves garlic, minced
- 1 red bell pepper, thinly sliced
- 1 cup sliced mushrooms
- 1 cup snow peas
- 1 cup broccoli florets
- 1/2 cup low-sodium vegetable broth
- 1/4 teaspoon red pepper flakes (optional for spice)
- Salt and pepper to taste

Directions:

- In a small bowl, whisk together the low-sodium soy sauce, rice vinegar, and cornstarch. Set aside.
- Heat the canola oil in a large skillet or wok over medium-high heat.
- Add the sliced onion and minced garlic to the skillet. Stir-fry for 2-3 minutes, or until the onion is tender and translucent.
- Add the sliced red bell pepper, mushrooms, snow peas, and broccoli florets to the skillet. Stir-fry for another 3-4 minutes, or until the vegetables are crisp-tender.
- Push the vegetables to one side of the skillet and add the shrimp to the other side. Cook the shrimp for 2-3 minutes, or until they turn pink and are cooked through.
- Pour the low-sodium sauce mixture over the shrimp and vegetables. Add the low-sodium

vegetable broth and red pepper flakes (if using). Stir everything together and cook for an additional 1-2 minutes, or until the sauce thickens slightly.

- Season with salt and pepper to taste.
- Serve the stir-fried shrimp and vegetables over cooked brown rice or quinoa.

Nutritional Information (per serving):

- Calories: 220
- Protein: 25g
- Fat: 5g
- Carbohydrates: 18g
- Fiber: 4g
- Sodium: 250mg
- Potassium: 450mg
- Phosphorus: 200mg

## TURKEY CHILI WITH KIDNEY BEANS AND LOW-SODIUM SEASONING

Time: 1 hour 30 minutes

Servings: 6

Ingredients:

- 1 pound lean ground turkey
- 1 onion, chopped
- 2 cloves garlic, minced
- 1 bell pepper, chopped
- 1 can (14 ounces) diced tomatoes, undrained
- 1 can (14 ounces) kidney beans, rinsed and drained
- 1 can (6 ounces) tomato paste
- 2 cups low-sodium chicken broth
- 2 teaspoons chili powder
- 1 teaspoon ground cumin
- 1/2 teaspoon paprika
- 1/2 teaspoon dried oregano
- 1/4 teaspoon cayenne pepper (optional for spice)
- Salt and pepper to taste

Directions:

- In a large pot, cook the ground turkey over medium heat until browned and cooked through. Drain any excess fat.
- Add the chopped onion, minced garlic, and chopped bell pepper to the pot. Cook for an additional 2-3 minutes, or until the vegetables are tender.
- Stir in the diced tomatoes, kidney beans, tomato paste, low-sodium chicken broth, chili powder, ground cumin, paprika, dried oregano, and cayenne pepper (if using).
- Bring the mixture to a boil, then reduce the heat to low. Simmer, covered, for 1 hour, stirring occasionally.
- Season with salt and pepper to taste.
- Serve the turkey chili hot, garnished with your choice of toppings such as chopped fresh cilantro, low-fat shredded cheese, or diced avocado.

Nutritional Information (per serving):

- Calories: 250
- Protein: 20g
- Fat: 6g
- Carbohydrates: 30g
- Fiber: 8g
- Sodium: 200mg
- Potassium: 600mg
- Phosphorus: 250mg

## BAKED EGGPLANT ROLLATINI WITH RICOTTA AND MARINARA SAUCE (LOW-SODIUM VERSION)

Time: 1 hour 15 minutes

Servings: 4

Ingredients:

- 2 medium eggplants, sliced lengthwise into 1/4-inch thick slices
- 2 cups low-sodium marinara sauce
- 1 cup part-skim ricotta cheese
- 1/2 cup grated Parmesan cheese
- 1/4 cup chopped fresh basil
- 1/4 cup chopped fresh parsley
- 2 cloves garlic, minced
- 1 egg, lightly beaten
- Salt and pepper to taste

Directions:

- Preheat the oven to 375°F (190°C). Line a baking sheet with parchment paper.
- Place the eggplant slices on the prepared baking sheet. Lightly brush both sides of the slices with olive oil. Season with salt and pepper.
- Bake the eggplant slices in the preheated oven for 20-25 minutes, or until they are tender and pliable. Remove from the oven and let them cool slightly.
- In a mixing bowl, combine the ricotta cheese, grated Parmesan cheese, chopped fresh basil, chopped fresh parsley, minced garlic, and the lightly beaten egg. Season with salt and pepper.
- Spread a thin layer of marinara sauce on the bottom of a baking dish.
- Lay an eggplant slice flat and spoon a tablespoon of the ricotta mixture onto one end of the slice. Roll up the eggplant slice, enclosing the filling, and place it seam-side down in the baking dish. Repeat with the remaining eggplant slices and ricotta mixture.
- Pour the remaining marinara sauce over the rolled eggplant slices in the baking dish.
- Bake in the oven for 25-30 minutes, or until the sauce is

bubbly and the cheese is melted and lightly browned.

- Remove from the oven and let it cool for a few minutes before serving.

Nutritional Information (per serving):

- Calories: 280
- Protein: 14g
- Fat: 12g
- Carbohydrates: 32g
- Fiber: 8g
- Sodium: 180mg
- Potassium: 600mg
- Phosphorus: 200mg

## GRILLED PORK TENDERLOIN WITH FRESH PINEAPPLE SALSA

Time: 1 hour

Servings: 4

Ingredients:

- 1 pound pork tenderloin
- 2 teaspoons olive oil
- 1 teaspoon ground cumin
- 1 teaspoon paprika
- 1/2 teaspoon garlic powder
- 1/2 teaspoon onion powder
- Salt and pepper to taste

*For the Fresh Pineapple Salsa:*

- 1 cup fresh pineapple, diced
- 1/2 red bell pepper, diced
- 1/4 red onion, finely chopped
- 1 jalapeno pepper, seeded and minced
- 2 tablespoons chopped fresh cilantro
- 1 tablespoon lime juice
- Salt to taste

Directions:

- Preheat the grill to medium-high heat.
- Rub the pork tenderloin with olive oil. In a small bowl, combine the ground cumin,

paprika, garlic powder, onion powder, salt, and pepper. Rub the spice mixture all over the pork tenderloin.
- Place the seasoned pork tenderloin on the preheated grill. Grill for about 15-20 minutes, turning occasionally, until the internal temperature reaches 145°F (63°C).
- While the pork is grilling, prepare the fresh pineapple salsa. In a bowl, combine the diced pineapple, diced red bell pepper, finely chopped red onion, minced jalapeno pepper, chopped fresh cilantro, lime juice, and salt. Mix well to combine.
- Remove the grilled pork tenderloin from the grill and let it rest for 5 minutes before slicing.
- Slice the pork tenderloin into medallions and serve with the fresh pineapple salsa.

Nutritional Information (per serving):

- Calories: 220
- Protein: 25g
- Fat: 8g
- Carbohydrates: 12g
- Fiber: 2g
- Sodium: 80mg
- Potassium: 500mg
- Phosphorus: 250mg

## QUINOA AND VEGETABLE STIR-FRY WITH LOW-SODIUM SOY SAUCE

Time: 30 minutes

Servings: 4

Ingredients:

- 1 cup quinoa, rinsed
- 2 cups low-sodium vegetable broth
- 1 tablespoon canola oil

- 1 onion, thinly sliced
- 2 cloves garlic, minced
- 1 bell pepper, thinly sliced
- 2 carrots, julienned
- 1 cup snap peas, trimmed
- 1 cup sliced mushrooms
- 2 tablespoons low-sodium soy sauce
- 1 tablespoon rice vinegar
- 1 teaspoon sesame oil
- Salt and pepper to taste
- Optional toppings: chopped green onions, sesame seeds

Directions:

- In a saucepan, bring the low-sodium vegetable broth to a boil. Add the rinsed quinoa and reduce the heat to low. Cover and simmer for 15-20 minutes, or until the quinoa is tender and the liquid is absorbed. Remove from heat and let it sit for 5 minutes. Fluff with a fork.
- Heat the canola oil in a large skillet or wok over medium-high heat.
- Add the thinly sliced onion and minced garlic to the skillet. Stir-fry for 2-3 minutes, or until the onion is tender and translucent.
- Add the thinly sliced bell pepper, julienned carrots, snap peas, and sliced mushrooms to the skillet. Stir-fry for another 3-4 minutes, or until the vegetables are crisp-tender.
- In a small bowl, whisk together the low-sodium soy sauce, rice vinegar, sesame oil, salt, and pepper. Pour the sauce over the stir-fried vegetables and toss to coat evenly.
- Add the cooked quinoa to the skillet and stir-fry for an additional 1-2 minutes, or until everything is heated through and well combined.

- Remove from heat and serve the quinoa and vegetable stir-fry hot. Optional: Garnish with chopped green onions and sesame seeds.

Nutritional Information (per serving):

- Calories: 280
- Protein: 10g
- Fat: 8g
- Carbohydrates: 45g
- Fiber: 8g
- Sodium: 200mg
- Potassium: 600mg
- Phosphorus: 250mg

## BAKED CHICKEN DRUMSTICKS WITH HERBS AND SPICES

Time: 1 hour

Servings: 4

Ingredients:

- 8 chicken drumsticks
- 2 tablespoons olive oil
- 1 teaspoon garlic powder
- 1 teaspoon dried thyme
- 1 teaspoon dried rosemary
- 1 teaspoon paprika
- Salt and pepper to taste

Directions:

- Preheat the oven to 425°F (220°C). Line a baking sheet with foil and place a wire rack on top.
- In a small bowl, mix together the garlic powder, dried thyme, dried rosemary, paprika, salt, and pepper.
- Pat the chicken drumsticks dry with paper towels. Rub the olive oil all over the drumsticks, then sprinkle the herb and spice mixture evenly over each drumstick, pressing gently to adhere.

- Place the seasoned drumsticks on the wire rack on the baking sheet.
- Bake in the preheated oven for 45-50 minutes, or until the chicken is golden brown and cooked through. The internal temperature should reach 165°F (74°C).
- Remove from the oven and let the chicken drumsticks rest for a few minutes before serving.

Nutritional Information (per serving):

- Calories: 250
- Protein: 28g
- Fat: 14g
- Carbohydrates: 1g
- Fiber: 0g
- Sodium: 150mg
- Potassium: 320mg
- Phosphorus: 210mg

## SPAGHETTI SQUASH WITH TURKEY BOLOGNESE SAUCE (LOW-SODIUM VERSION)

Time: 1 hour 30 minutes

Servings: 4

Ingredients:

- 1 medium spaghetti squash
- 1 pound ground turkey
- 1 onion, finely chopped
- 2 cloves garlic, minced
- 1 carrot, finely chopped
- 1 celery stalk, finely chopped
- 1 can (14 ounces) diced tomatoes, undrained
- 1 can (6 ounces) tomato paste
- 1/2 cup low-sodium chicken broth
- 1 teaspoon dried basil
- 1 teaspoon dried oregano
- 1/2 teaspoon dried thyme
- 1/4 teaspoon red pepper flakes (optional for spice)
- Salt and pepper to taste

Directions:

- Preheat the oven to 400°F (200°C). Cut the spaghetti squash in half lengthwise and scoop out the seeds.
- Place the spaghetti squash halves cut side down on a baking sheet. Bake in the preheated oven for 40-45 minutes, or until the squash is tender. Let it cool slightly, then use a fork to scrape out the spaghetti-like strands.
- While the spaghetti squash is baking, prepare the turkey bolognese sauce. In a large skillet, cook the ground turkey over medium heat until browned and cooked through. Drain any excess fat.
- Add the finely chopped onion, minced garlic, finely chopped carrot, and finely chopped celery to the skillet. Cook for an additional 2-3 minutes, or until the vegetables are tender.
- Stir in the diced tomatoes, tomato paste, low-sodium chicken broth, dried basil, dried oregano, dried thyme, and red pepper flakes (if using). Simmer the sauce for 30-40 minutes, stirring occasionally. Season with salt and pepper to taste.
- Serve the spaghetti squash with the turkey bolognese sauce on top. Optional: Garnish with chopped fresh basil or grated Parmesan cheese.

Nutritional Information (per serving):

- Calories: 220
- Protein: 20g
- Fat: 8g
- Carbohydrates: 18g
- Fiber: 4g
- Sodium: 180mg
- Potassium: 550mg

- Phosphorus: 210mg

# CHAPTER 10: DELICIOUS SIDES AND SNACKS

## ROASTED BRUSSELS SPROUTS WITH LEMON AND GARLIC

Time: 30 minutes

Servings: 4

Ingredients:

- 1 pound Brussels sprouts, trimmed and halved
- 2 tablespoons olive oil
- 2 cloves garlic, minced
- 1 lemon, zested and juiced
- Salt and pepper to taste

Directions:

- Preheat the oven to 400°F (200°C).
- In a mixing bowl, toss the Brussels sprouts with olive oil, minced garlic, lemon zest, lemon juice, salt, and pepper.
- Spread the Brussels sprouts evenly on a baking sheet.
- Roast in the preheated oven for 20-25 minutes, or until the sprouts are tender and lightly browned.
- Remove from the oven and serve hot.

Nutritional Information:

- Calories: 90
- Carbohydrates: 10g
- Protein: 4g
- Fat: 5g
- Fiber: 4g
- Sodium: 20mg
- Potassium: 400mg
- Phosphorus: 80mg

## BAKED SWEET POTATO FRIES WITH LOW-SODIUM SEASONING

Time: 40 minutes

Servings: 4

Ingredients:

- 2 large sweet potatoes, peeled and cut into fries
- 1 tablespoon olive oil
- 1 teaspoon low-sodium seasoning blend (e.g., herbs, spices, and salt-free seasoning)
- Salt and pepper to taste

Directions:

- Preheat the oven to 425°F (220°C).
- In a mixing bowl, toss the sweet potato fries with olive oil, low-sodium seasoning blend, salt, and pepper.
- Spread the fries in a single layer on a baking sheet.
- Bake in the preheated oven for 25-30 minutes, or until the fries are crispy and golden brown.
- Remove from the oven and let cool for a few minutes before serving.

Nutritional Information:

- Calories: 150
- Carbohydrates: 31g
- Protein: 2g
- Fat: 3g
- Fiber: 5g
- Sodium: 30mg
- Potassium: 400mg
- Phosphorus: 70mg

## STEAMED GREEN BEANS WITH ALMONDS

Time: 15 minutes

Servings: 4

Ingredients:

- 1 pound green beans, ends trimmed
- 2 tablespoons slivered almonds
- 1 tablespoon olive oil
- 1 teaspoon lemon juice
- Salt and pepper to taste

Directions:

- Fill a pot with water and bring it to a boil.
- Add the green beans to the boiling water and cook for 3-5 minutes, or until they are crisp-tender.
- Drain the green beans and transfer them to a serving bowl.
- In a small skillet, toast the slivered almonds over medium heat until golden brown.
- In a separate bowl, whisk together olive oil, lemon juice, salt, and pepper.
- Drizzle the olive oil mixture over the steamed green beans and toss gently to coat.
- Sprinkle the toasted almonds over the top.
- Serve warm.

Nutritional Information:

- Calories: 70
- Carbohydrates: 6g
- Protein: 2g
- Fat: 5g
- Fiber: 3g
- Sodium: 10mg
- Potassium: 200mg
- Phosphorus: 45mg

## GUACAMOLE WITH FRESH VEGETABLES FOR DIPPING

Time: 10 minutes

Servings: 4

Ingredients:

- 2 ripe avocados, peeled and pitted
- 1 small tomato, diced
- 1/4 cup red onion, finely chopped
- 1/4 cup fresh cilantro, chopped
- 1 jalapeno pepper, seeds removed and finely chopped
- 1 lime, juiced
- Salt and pepper to taste
- Assorted fresh vegetables (such as cucumber slices, bell pepper strips, and carrot sticks) for dipping

Directions:

- In a bowl, mash the avocados with a fork until smooth.
- Add the diced tomato, red onion, cilantro, jalapeno pepper, lime juice, salt, and pepper to the bowl.
- Stir well to combine all the ingredients.
- Taste and adjust the seasoning if needed.
- Serve the guacamole with fresh vegetable slices for dipping.

Nutritional Information:

- Calories: 160
- Carbohydrates: 10g
- Protein: 2g
- Fat: 15g
- Fiber: 7g
- Sodium: 10mg
- Potassium: 480mg
- Phosphorus: 60mg

## KALE CHIPS WITH OLIVE OIL AND SEA SALT

Time: 25 minutes

Servings: 4

Ingredients:

- 1 bunch kale, stems removed and torn into bite-sized pieces
- 1 tablespoon olive oil
- Sea salt to taste

## Directions:

- Preheat the oven to 350°F (175°C).
- In a large bowl, toss the kale pieces with olive oil until well coated.
- Spread the kale evenly on a baking sheet lined with parchment paper.
- Sprinkle with sea salt to taste.
- Bake in the preheated oven for 12-15 minutes, or until the kale chips are crispy and lightly browned.
- Remove from the oven and let cool before serving.

## Nutritional Information:

- Calories: 50
- Carbohydrates: 5g
- Protein: 2g
- Fat: 3g
- Fiber: 2g
- Sodium: 100mg
- Potassium: 230mg
- Phosphorus: 50mg

## BAKED PARMESAN ZUCCHINI FRIES (LOW-SODIUM VERSION)

Time: 35 minutes

Servings: 4

## Ingredients:

- 2 medium zucchini, cut into fries
- 1/4 cup grated Parmesan cheese
- 1/4 cup breadcrumbs (preferably low-sodium)
- 1/2 teaspoon garlic powder
- 1/2 teaspoon paprika
- Salt and pepper to taste
- Cooking spray

## Directions:

- Preheat the oven to 425°F (220°C).

- In a shallow dish, combine the Parmesan cheese, breadcrumbs, garlic powder, paprika, salt, and pepper.
- Dip each zucchini fry into the mixture, pressing gently to coat all sides.
- Place the coated zucchini fries on a baking sheet lined with parchment paper.
- Lightly spray the fries with cooking spray.
- Bake in the preheated oven for 20-25 minutes, or until the fries are golden and crispy.
- Remove from the oven and serve hot.

Nutritional Information:

- Calories: 90
- Carbohydrates: 11g
- Protein: 6g
- Fat: 3g
- Fiber: 2g
- Sodium: 80mg
- Potassium: 300mg
- Phosphorus: 100mg

## SLICED CUCUMBER WITH HUMMUS

Time: 10 minutes

Servings: 4

Ingredients:

- 2 medium cucumbers, sliced
- 1/2 cup low-sodium hummus

Directions:

- Wash the cucumbers and slice them into rounds or sticks.
- Arrange the cucumber slices on a serving platter.
- Place the hummus in a small bowl as a dipping sauce.
- Serve the cucumber slices with the hummus on the side.

Nutritional Information:

- Calories: 70

- Carbohydrates: 10g
- Protein: 4g
- Fat: 2g
- Fiber: 2g
- Sodium: 60mg
- Potassium: 300mg
- Phosphorus: 70mg

## ROASTED CAULIFLOWER WITH TURMERIC AND CUMIN

Time: 30 minutes

Servings: 4

Ingredients:

- 1 medium head cauliflower, cut into florets
- 2 tablespoons olive oil
- 1 teaspoon ground turmeric
- 1 teaspoon ground cumin
- Salt and pepper to taste

Directions:

- Preheat the oven to 425°F (220°C).
- In a large bowl, combine the cauliflower florets, olive oil, turmeric, cumin, salt, and pepper. Toss until the cauliflower is evenly coated.
- Spread the cauliflower on a baking sheet lined with parchment paper.
- Roast in the preheated oven for 25-30 minutes, or until the cauliflower is tender and golden brown.
- Remove from the oven and let cool slightly before serving.

Nutritional Information:

- Calories: 80
- Carbohydrates: 8g
- Protein: 3g
- Fat: 5g
- Fiber: 4g
- Sodium: 40mg
- Potassium: 400mg

- Phosphorus: 70mg

## POPCORN SEASONED WITH NUTRITIONAL YEAST (LOW-SODIUM VERSION)

Time: 10 minutes

Servings: 4

Ingredients:

- 1/2 cup popcorn kernels
- 2 tablespoons nutritional yeast
- 1 tablespoon melted unsalted butter (optional)
- Salt to taste

Directions:

- Pop the popcorn kernels using an air popper or stovetop method.
- In a small bowl, combine the nutritional yeast and salt.
- Drizzle the melted butter over the popped popcorn (if using) and toss to coat.
- Sprinkle the nutritional yeast mixture over the popcorn and toss again to distribute the seasoning.
- Serve immediately.

Nutritional Information:

- Calories: 80
- Carbohydrates: 14g
- Protein: 3g
- Fat: 2g
- Fiber: 3g
- Sodium: 20mg
- Potassium: 70mg
- Phosphorus: 50mg

## GREEK YOGURT AND VEGGIE DIP WITH BELL PEPPER STRIPS

Time: 10 minutes

Servings: 4

Ingredients:

- 1 cup plain Greek yogurt (low-fat)
- 1/4 cup finely chopped mixed vegetables (such as cucumber, bell pepper, and carrot)
- 1 tablespoon fresh lemon juice
- 1 tablespoon chopped fresh dill (optional)
- Salt and pepper to taste
- Bell pepper strips for dipping

Directions:

- In a bowl, combine the Greek yogurt, chopped mixed vegetables, lemon juice, chopped fresh dill, salt, and pepper. Stir well to combine.
- Transfer the dip to a serving bowl.
- Serve the Greek yogurt and veggie dip with bell pepper strips for dipping.

Nutritional Information:

- Calories: 70
- Carbohydrates: 6g
- Protein: 8g
- Fat: 1g
- Fiber: 1g
- Sodium: 40mg
- Potassium: 180mg
- Phosphorus: 70mg

## QUINOA SALAD WITH DICED TOMATOES AND CUCUMBERS

Time: 20 minutes

Servings: 4

Ingredients:

- 1 cup cooked quinoa
- 1 cup diced tomatoes
- 1 cup diced cucumbers
- 2 tablespoons chopped fresh parsley
- 1 tablespoon extra virgin olive oil
- 1 tablespoon lemon juice
- Salt and pepper to taste

## Directions:

- In a large bowl, combine the cooked quinoa, diced tomatoes, diced cucumbers, chopped parsley, olive oil, lemon juice, salt, and pepper.
- Toss well to combine all the ingredients.
- Adjust the seasoning if needed.
- Let the salad sit for a few minutes to allow the flavors to meld.
- Serve at room temperature or chilled.

## Nutritional Information:

- Calories: 130
- Carbohydrates: 20g
- Protein: 4g
- Fat: 5g
- Fiber: 3g
- Sodium: 10mg
- Potassium: 260mg
- Phosphorus: 80mg

## OVEN-BAKED BEET CHIPS WITH HERBS AND SPICES

Time: 40 minutes

Servings: 4

Ingredients:

- 2 large beets, peeled and thinly sliced
- 1 tablespoon olive oil
- 1/2 teaspoon dried thyme
- 1/2 teaspoon paprika
- Salt and pepper to taste

Directions:

- Preheat the oven to 350°F (175°C).
- In a large bowl, toss the beet slices with olive oil, dried thyme, paprika, salt, and pepper until well coated.
- Arrange the beet slices in a single layer on a baking sheet lined with parchment paper.

- Bake in the preheated oven for 30-35 minutes, or until the beet chips are crisp and slightly curled.
- Remove from the oven and let cool before serving.

Nutritional Information:

- Calories: 70
- Carbohydrates: 10g
- Protein: 1g
- Fat: 3g
- Fiber: 3g
- Sodium: 80mg
- Potassium: 280mg
- Phosphorus: 40mg

## SLICED APPLE WITH ALMOND BUTTER

Time: 5 minutes

Servings: 4

Ingredients:

- 2 medium apples, sliced
- 4 tablespoons almond butter (unsweetened)

Directions:

- Wash the apples and slice them into thin rounds or wedges.
- Arrange the apple slices on a plate.
- Serve the sliced apples with almond butter for dipping.

Nutritional Information:

- Calories: 150
- Carbohydrates: 20g
- Protein: 4g
- Fat: 8g
- Fiber: 4g
- Sodium: 0mg
- Potassium: 200mg
- Phosphorus: 80mg

## STEAMED EDAMAME WITH SEA SALT (LOW-SODIUM VERSION)

Time: 10 minutes

Servings: 4

Ingredients:

- 2 cups frozen edamame (shelled)
- 1 teaspoon sea salt

Directions:

- Bring a pot of water to a boil.
- Add the frozen edamame to the boiling water and cook for 4-5 minutes, or until the edamame is tender.
- Drain the edamame and transfer to a serving bowl.
- Sprinkle with sea salt and toss to coat.
- Serve warm.

Nutritional Information:

- Calories: 120
- Carbohydrates: 9g
- Protein: 10g
- Fat: 4g
- Fiber: 5g
- Sodium: 20mg
- Potassium: 400mg
- Phosphorus: 140mg

## CARROT AND CELERY STICKS WITH LOW-SODIUM RANCH DRESSING

Time: 10 minutes

Servings: 4

Ingredients:

- 2 large carrots, peeled and cut into sticks
- 2 celery stalks, cut into sticks
- 1/2 cup low-sodium ranch dressing

Directions:

- Arrange the carrot and celery sticks on a plate.
- Serve the carrot and celery sticks with low-sodium ranch dressing for dipping.

Nutritional Information:

- Calories: 80
- Carbohydrates: 8g
- Protein: 1g
- Fat: 5g
- Fiber: 2g
- Sodium: 60mg
- Potassium: 300mg
- Phosphorus: 40mg

## ROASTED EGGPLANT DIP WITH WHOLE WHEAT PITA BREAD (LOW-SODIUM VERSION)

Time: 50 minutes

Servings: 4

Ingredients:

- 1 large eggplant
- 2 tablespoons olive oil
- 1 clove garlic, minced
- 1 tablespoon lemon juice
- 1 tablespoon chopped fresh parsley
- Salt and pepper to taste
- Whole wheat pita bread, cut into triangles, for serving

Directions:

- Preheat the oven to 400°F (200°C).
- Prick the eggplant with a fork in several places and place it on a baking sheet.
- Roast the eggplant in the preheated oven for 40-45 minutes, or until it becomes soft and collapses.
- Remove the eggplant from the oven and let it cool slightly.
- Cut the eggplant in half and scoop out the flesh into a bowl, discarding the skin.

- Mash the roasted eggplant with a fork until smooth.
- Add the olive oil, minced garlic, lemon juice, chopped parsley, salt, and pepper to the bowl. Stir well to combine.
- Adjust the seasoning if needed.
- Serve the roasted eggplant dip with whole wheat pita bread triangles.

Nutritional Information:

- Calories: 90
- Carbohydrates: 11g
- Protein: 2g
- Fat: 5g
- Fiber: 4g
- Sodium: 10mg
- Potassium: 250mg
- Phosphorus: 40mg

## ROASTED BUTTERNUT SQUASH WITH CINNAMON AND NUTMEG

Time: 40 minutes

Servings: 4

Ingredients:

- 1 small butternut squash, peeled, seeded, and cut into cubes
- 1 tablespoon olive oil
- 1 teaspoon ground cinnamon
- 1/2 teaspoon ground nutmeg
- Salt and pepper to taste

Directions:

- Preheat the oven to 400°F (200°C).
- In a bowl, toss the butternut squash cubes with olive oil, cinnamon, nutmeg, salt, and pepper until evenly coated.
- Spread the butternut squash on a baking sheet lined with parchment paper.

- Roast in the preheated oven for 30-35 minutes, or until the squash is tender and caramelized.
- Remove from the oven and let cool slightly before serving.

Nutritional Information:

- Calories: 80
- Carbohydrates: 18g
- Protein: 2g
- Fat: 2g
- Fiber: 4g
- Sodium: 5mg
- Potassium: 570mg
- Phosphorus: 50mg

## ZUCCHINI NOODLES WITH LOW-SODIUM MARINARA SAUCE

Time: 20 minutes

Servings: 4

Ingredients:

- 4 medium zucchini
- 2 cups low-sodium marinara sauce
- Fresh basil leaves for garnish

Directions:

- Using a spiralizer or vegetable peeler, create noodles from the zucchini.
- In a large non-stick pan, heat the marinara sauce over medium heat until warmed through.
- Add the zucchini noodles to the pan and toss gently to coat them with the sauce.
- Cook for 3-5 minutes, or until the zucchini noodles are tender but still have a slight crunch.
- Remove from the heat and garnish with fresh basil leaves before serving.

Nutritional Information:

- Calories: 70
- Carbohydrates: 12g

- Protein: 3g
- Fat: 2g
- Fiber: 3g
- Sodium: 70mg
- Potassium: 500mg
- Phosphorus: 60mg

## BAKED CHICKPEA SNACK WITH PAPRIKA AND CUMIN

Time: 40 minutes

Servings: 4

Ingredients:

- 2 cups cooked chickpeas (canned or cooked from dry)
- 1 tablespoon olive oil
- 1 teaspoon paprika
- 1/2 teaspoon ground cumin
- Salt and pepper to taste

Directions:

- Preheat the oven to 400°F (200°C).
- Rinse and drain the chickpeas, then pat them dry with a paper towel.
- In a bowl, toss the chickpeas with olive oil, paprika, cumin, salt, and pepper until evenly coated.
- Spread the chickpeas on a baking sheet lined with parchment paper.
- Bake in the preheated oven for 30-35 minutes, or until the chickpeas are golden brown and crispy.
- Remove from the oven and let cool before serving.

Nutritional Information:

- Calories: 150
- Carbohydrates: 24g
- Protein: 7g
- Fat: 4g
- Fiber: 7g
- Sodium: 10mg
- Potassium: 240mg
- Phosphorus: 100mg

## GRILLED PORTOBELLO MUSHROOMS WITH BALSAMIC GLAZE

Time: 20 minutes

Servings: 4

Ingredients:

- 4 large Portobello mushroom caps
- 2 tablespoons balsamic vinegar
- 1 tablespoon olive oil
- 2 cloves garlic, minced
- Salt and pepper to taste
- Fresh parsley for garnish

Directions:

- Preheat the grill to medium heat.
- In a small bowl, whisk together the balsamic vinegar, olive oil, minced garlic, salt, and pepper.
- Brush both sides of the mushroom caps with the balsamic mixture.
- Place the mushroom caps on the grill, gill-side down, and cook for 4-5 minutes.
- Flip the mushroom caps and continue grilling for an additional 4-5 minutes, or until the mushrooms are tender and juicy.
- Remove from the grill and garnish with fresh parsley before serving.

Nutritional Information:

- Calories: 60
- Carbohydrates: 8g
- Protein: 4g
- Fat: 2g
- Fiber: 2g
- Sodium: 10mg
- Potassium: 460mg
- Phosphorus: 80mg

# CHAPTER 11: DELECTABLE DESSERTS FOR DIABETIC RENAL DIETS

## BERRY PARFAIT WITH SUGAR-FREE WHIPPED CREAM AND CHOPPED NUTS

Time: 10 minutes

Servings: 2

Ingredients:

- 1 cup mixed berries (strawberries, blueberries, raspberries)
- 1 cup sugar-free whipped cream
- 2 tablespoons chopped nuts (such as almonds or walnuts)

Directions:

- Rinse the mixed berries and pat them dry with a paper towel.
- In two serving glasses or bowls, layer the mixed berries alternately with sugar-free whipped cream.
- Sprinkle the chopped nuts on top.
- Serve immediately and enjoy!

Nutritional Information:

- Calories: 120
- Carbohydrates: 8g
- Protein: 2g
- Fat: 9g
- Sodium: 5mg
- Potassium: 100mg
- Phosphorus: 45mg

## BAKED APPLES WITH CINNAMON AND GREEK YOGURT

Time: 40 minutes

Servings: 4

Ingredients:

- 4 medium-sized apples
- 1 teaspoon cinnamon
- 1/4 cup Greek yogurt (unsweetened)

Directions:

- Preheat the oven to 350°F (175°C).
- Wash the apples and remove the cores, leaving the bottoms intact.
- Place the apples in a baking dish and sprinkle cinnamon evenly over each apple.
- Bake in the preheated oven for about 30 minutes or until the apples are tender.
- Remove from the oven and allow them to cool slightly.
- Serve each apple with a dollop of Greek yogurt on top.
- Enjoy warm or chilled.

Nutritional Information:

- Calories: 100
- Carbohydrates: 20g
- Protein: 2g
- Fat: 0.5g
- Sodium: 10mg
- Potassium: 150mg
- Phosphorus: 30mg

## CHOCOLATE AVOCADO MOUSSE WITH STEVIA

Time: 15 minutes

Servings: 4

Ingredients:

- 2 ripe avocados

- 1/4 cup unsweetened cocoa powder
- 1/4 cup almond milk (unsweetened)
- 2-3 tablespoons stevia (or sweetener of your choice)
- 1 teaspoon vanilla extract

Directions:

- Cut the avocados in half, remove the pits, and scoop the flesh into a blender or food processor.
- Add cocoa powder, almond milk, stevia, and vanilla extract to the blender.
- Blend until smooth and creamy, scraping down the sides as needed.
- Taste and adjust the sweetness if desired by adding more stevia.
- Transfer the mousse to individual serving dishes or ramekins.
- Refrigerate for at least 1 hour before serving.
- Garnish with a sprinkle of cocoa powder or a dollop of sugar-free whipped cream, if desired.
- Enjoy chilled.

Nutritional Information:

- Calories: 150
- Carbohydrates: 10g
- Protein: 3g
- Fat: 13g
- Sodium: 10mg
- Potassium: 350mg
- Phosphorus: 80mg

## SUGAR-FREE LEMON BARS WITH ALMOND FLOUR CRUST

Time: 1 hour 30 minutes

Servings: 9

Ingredients:

*For the crust:*

- 1 cup almond flour
- 1/4 cup coconut flour

- 2 tablespoons melted coconut oil
- 2 tablespoons unsweetened almond milk
- 2 tablespoons stevia (or sweetener of your choice)
- Pinch of salt

*For the lemon filling:*

- 1/2 cup fresh lemon juice
- 1 tablespoon lemon zest
- 1/2 cup stevia (or sweetener of your choice)
- 3 large eggs
- 2 tablespoons almond flour
- 1/4 teaspoon baking powder
- Powdered stevia (for dusting, optional)

Directions:

- Preheat the oven to 350°F (175°C) and line an 8x8-inch baking dish with parchment paper.
- In a mixing bowl, combine almond flour, coconut flour, melted coconut oil, almond milk, stevia, and a pinch of salt. Mix well until a dough forms.
- Press the dough evenly into the bottom of the prepared baking dish to form the crust.
- Bake the crust in the preheated oven for 12-15 minutes or until golden brown. Remove from the oven and set aside.
- In a separate bowl, whisk together lemon juice, lemon zest, stevia, eggs, almond flour, and baking powder until well combined.
- Pour the lemon filling over the baked crust and spread it evenly.
- Return the dish to the oven and bake for an additional 18-20 minutes or until the filling is set.
- Remove from the oven and let it cool completely before cutting into squares.
- Dust with powdered stevia, if desired, before serving.

- Enjoy these delightful sugar-free lemon bars!

Nutritional Information:

- Calories: 120
- Carbohydrates: 7g
- Protein: 4g
- Fat: 9g
- Sodium: 60mg
- Potassium: 80mg
- Phosphorus: 70mg

## CHIA SEED PUDDING WITH UNSWEETENED COCOA POWDER AND FRESH BERRIES

Time: 6 hours (including chilling time)

Servings: 2

Ingredients:

- 1/4 cup chia seeds
- 1 cup unsweetened almond milk
- 2 tablespoons unsweetened cocoa powder
- 2 tablespoons stevia (or sweetener of your choice)
- 1/2 teaspoon vanilla extract
- Fresh berries (such as strawberries, blueberries, or raspberries) for topping

Directions:

- In a bowl, combine chia seeds, almond milk, cocoa powder, stevia, and vanilla extract.
- Stir well until all the ingredients are thoroughly mixed.
- Let the mixture sit for 5 minutes, then stir again to prevent clumping of the chia seeds.
- Cover the bowl and refrigerate for at least 6 hours or overnight to allow the chia seeds to absorb the liquid and form a pudding-like consistency.

- Once the chia pudding has set, give it a good stir to break up any clumps.
- Divide the pudding into serving bowls or glasses.
- Top with fresh berries.
- Serve chilled and enjoy this creamy and nutritious chia seed pudding.

Nutritional Information:

- Calories: 100
- Carbohydrates: 10g
- Protein: 4g
- Fat: 6g
- Sodium: 80mg
- Potassium: 120mg
- Phosphorus: 120mg

## GRILLED PINEAPPLE WITH CINNAMON AND LOW-SUGAR ICE CREAM

Time: 20 minutes

Servings: 4

Ingredients:

- 1 small pineapple, peeled and cored
- 1 teaspoon cinnamon
- 2 tablespoons stevia (or sweetener of your choice)
- Low-sugar vanilla ice cream (or frozen yogurt) for serving

Directions:

- Preheat the grill to medium-high heat.
- Cut the pineapple into slices or wedges.
- In a small bowl, combine cinnamon and stevia.
- Sprinkle the cinnamon mixture evenly over both sides of the pineapple slices.
- Place the pineapple slices on the preheated grill and cook for about 3-4 minutes per side, or

until grill marks appear and the pineapple is slightly softened.
- Remove the grilled pineapple from the grill and let it cool for a few minutes.
- Serve the grilled pineapple with a scoop of low-sugar vanilla ice cream.
- Enjoy this delightful and guilt-free dessert!

Nutritional Information:

- Calories: 80
- Carbohydrates: 20g
- Protein: 1g
- Fat: 0.5g
- Sodium: 0mg
- Potassium: 150mg
- Phosphorus: 20mg

## BANANA ICE CREAM WITH ALMOND MILK AND UNSWEETENED COCOA POWDER

Time: 5 minutes

Servings: 2

Ingredients:

- 2 ripe bananas, sliced and frozen
- 1/4 cup unsweetened almond milk
- 1 tablespoon unsweetened cocoa powder
- 1/2 teaspoon vanilla extract
- Optional toppings: chopped nuts, grated dark chocolate

Directions:

- Place the frozen banana slices, almond milk, cocoa powder, and vanilla extract in a blender or food processor.
- Blend until smooth and creamy, scraping down the sides as needed.
- If the mixture is too thick, add a little more almond milk to achieve the desired consistency.

- Transfer the banana ice cream to bowls.
- Add your favorite toppings, such as chopped nuts or grated dark chocolate.
- Serve immediately and enjoy this guilt-free frozen treat!

Nutritional Information:

- Calories: 90
- Carbohydrates: 20g
- Protein: 2g
- Fat: 1g
- Sodium: 10mg
- Potassium: 350mg
- Phosphorus: 40mg

## LOW-SODIUM STRAWBERRY SHORTCAKE WITH WHOLE WHEAT BISCUITS

Time: 30 minutes

Servings: 6

Ingredients:

*For the biscuits:*

- 1 1/2 cups whole wheat flour
- 2 tablespoons stevia (or sweetener of your choice)
- 2 teaspoons baking powder
- 1/4 teaspoon salt
- 1/4 cup cold unsalted butter, cut into small pieces
- 1/2 cup unsweetened almond milk

*For the strawberry filling:*

- 3 cups fresh strawberries, hulled and sliced
- 2 tablespoons stevia (or sweetener of your choice)
- 1/2 teaspoon vanilla extract

*For the whipped cream:*

- 1 cup heavy cream
- 2 tablespoons stevia (or sweetener of your choice)
- 1/2 teaspoon vanilla extract

Directions:

- Preheat the oven to 400°F (200°C).
- In a mixing bowl, combine whole wheat flour, stevia, baking powder, and salt.
- Add the cold butter to the flour mixture and cut it in using a pastry cutter or your fingers until the mixture resembles coarse crumbs.
- Pour in the almond milk and stir until just combined, being careful not to overmix.
- Turn the dough out onto a lightly floured surface and gently knead it a few times until it comes together.
- Roll out the dough to about 1/2-inch thickness.
- Use a round biscuit cutter to cut out biscuits and place them on a baking sheet lined with parchment paper.
- Bake in the preheated oven for 12-15 minutes or until the biscuits are golden brown.
- While the biscuits are baking, prepare the strawberry filling by combining sliced strawberries, stevia, and vanilla extract in a bowl. Toss gently to coat the strawberries and set aside.
- In a separate mixing bowl, whip the heavy cream, stevia, and vanilla extract until stiff peaks form.
- Once the biscuits have cooled slightly, split them in half horizontally.
- Place the bottom halves of the biscuits on serving plates and spoon a generous amount of strawberry filling on top.
- Top with a dollop of whipped cream and cover with the remaining biscuit halves.

- Serve immediately and enjoy this delightful low-sodium strawberry shortcake!

Nutritional Information:

- Calories: 240
- Carbohydrates: 22g
- Protein: 5g
- Fat: 15g
- Sodium: 70mg
- Potassium: 280mg
- Phosphorus: 120mg

## BAKED PEARS WITH WALNUTS AND CINNAMON

Time: 30 minutes

Servings: 4

Ingredients:

- 4 ripe pears, halved and cored
- 2 tablespoons chopped walnuts
- 1 tablespoon stevia (or sweetener of your choice)
- 1 teaspoon ground cinnamon
- 1/4 teaspoon nutmeg (optional)
- 1/2 cup water

Directions:

- Preheat the oven to 375°F (190°C).
- Place the pear halves, cut side up, in a baking dish.
- In a small bowl, combine chopped walnuts, stevia, cinnamon, and nutmeg.
- Sprinkle the walnut mixture evenly over the pear halves.
- Pour water into the bottom of the baking dish.
- Cover the baking dish with foil and bake in the preheated oven for 20-25 minutes or until the pears are tender.
- Remove the foil and continue baking for an additional 5 minutes to allow the topping to crisp up slightly.

- Remove from the oven and let the baked pears cool for a few minutes before serving.
- Serve the baked pears warm as a delicious and healthy dessert.

Nutritional Information:

- Calories: 120
- Carbohydrates: 20g
- Protein: 2g
- Fat: 4g
- Sodium: 0mg
- Potassium: 230mg
- Phosphorus: 40mg

## SUGAR-FREE CHEESECAKE WITH ALMOND FLOUR CRUST

Time: 1 hour 30 minutes (plus chilling time)

Servings: 8

Ingredients:

*For the crust:*

- 1 1/2 cups almond flour
- 2 tablespoons melted coconut oil
- 2 tablespoons stevia (or sweetener of your choice)
- 1/2 teaspoon vanilla extract

*For the filling:*

- 2 cups cream cheese, softened
- 1/2 cup stevia (or sweetener of your choice)
- 2 large eggs
- 1 teaspoon vanilla extract
- 1 tablespoon lemon juice
- Optional toppings: fresh berries, sugar-free whipped cream

Directions:

- Preheat the oven to 325°F (165°C) and grease a 9-inch springform pan.
- In a mixing bowl, combine almond flour, melted coconut oil, stevia, and vanilla extract for the crust. Mix well until the mixture resembles coarse crumbs.

- Press the crust mixture evenly onto the bottom of the prepared springform pan.
- Bake the crust in the preheated oven for 10 minutes. Remove from the oven and set aside.
- In a separate mixing bowl, beat the cream cheese and stevia until smooth and creamy.
- Add eggs, one at a time, beating well after each addition.
- Stir in vanilla extract and lemon juice until well combined.
- Pour the filling over the baked crust in the springform pan.
- Smooth the top with a spatula.
- Bake in the preheated oven for 50-55 minutes or until the center is set and the edges are slightly golden.
- Turn off the oven and leave the cheesecake in the oven with the door slightly ajar for about 1 hour to cool slowly.
- Remove the cheesecake from the oven and let it cool completely before refrigerating for at least 4 hours or overnight to set.
- Once chilled and set, remove the cheesecake from the springform pan.
- Slice and serve with fresh berries and sugar-free whipped cream, if desired.
- Enjoy this indulgent sugar-free cheesecake!

Nutritional Information:

- Calories: 270
- Carbohydrates: 6g
- Protein: 8g
- Fat: 24g
- Sodium: 170mg
- Potassium: 150mg
- Phosphorus: 130mg

## GREEK YOGURT BARK WITH SUGAR-FREE DARK CHOCOLATE AND NUTS

Time: 2 hours 30 minutes (including freezing time)

Servings: 8

Ingredients:

- 2 cups plain Greek yogurt
- 2 tablespoons stevia (or sweetener of your choice)
- 1 teaspoon vanilla extract
- 2 ounces sugar-free dark chocolate, chopped
- 2 tablespoons chopped nuts (such as almonds, walnuts, or pistachios)

Directions:

- In a mixing bowl, combine Greek yogurt, stevia, and vanilla extract. Stir well to combine.
- Line a baking sheet with parchment paper.
- Spread the Greek yogurt mixture evenly onto the prepared baking sheet.
- Sprinkle the chopped dark chocolate and nuts over the yogurt mixture, pressing them gently into the surface.
- Place the baking sheet in the freezer and freeze for at least 2 hours or until the yogurt bark is firm.
- Once frozen, break the bark into pieces of desired size and serve immediately.
- Enjoy this refreshing and guilt-free treat!

Nutritional Information:

- Calories: 70
- Carbohydrates: 5g
- Protein: 6g
- Fat: 4g
- Sodium: 30mg
- Potassium: 110mg
- Phosphorus: 70mg

## PUMPKIN SPICE MUFFINS WITH ALMOND FLOUR AND STEVIA

Time: 35 minutes

Servings: 12

Ingredients:

- 2 cups almond flour
- 1/2 cup stevia (or sweetener of your choice)
- 2 teaspoons baking powder
- 1/2 teaspoon baking soda
- 1/2 teaspoon ground cinnamon
- 1/4 teaspoon ground nutmeg
- 1/4 teaspoon ground ginger
- 1/4 teaspoon ground cloves
- 1/4 teaspoon salt
- 1 cup pumpkin puree
- 3 large eggs
- 1/4 cup unsweetened almond milk
- 1 teaspoon vanilla extract

Directions:

- Preheat the oven to 350°F (175°C). Line a muffin tin with paper liners.
- In a mixing bowl, whisk together almond flour, stevia, baking powder, baking soda, cinnamon, nutmeg, ginger, cloves, and salt.
- In a separate bowl, whisk together pumpkin puree, eggs, almond milk, and vanilla extract until well combined.
- Add the wet ingredients to the dry ingredients and stir until just combined, being careful not to overmix.
- Spoon the batter into the prepared muffin tin, filling each cup about 3/4 full.
- Bake in the preheated oven for 20-25 minutes or until a toothpick inserted into the center of a muffin comes out clean.

- Remove from the oven and let the muffins cool in the tin for 5 minutes, then transfer them to a wire rack to cool completely.
- Once cooled, the muffins are ready to be enjoyed. Store any leftovers in an airtight container.

Nutritional Information:

- Calories: 120
- Carbohydrates: 6g
- Protein: 5g
- Fat: 10g
- Sodium: 180mg
- Potassium: 130mg
- Phosphorus: 90mg

## RASPBERRY SORBET WITH FRESH MINT LEAVES

Time: 3 hours 30 minutes (including freezing time)

Servings: 4

Ingredients:

- 4 cups frozen raspberries
- 1/4 cup water
- 2 tablespoons stevia (or sweetener of your choice)
- Fresh mint leaves for garnish

Directions:

- In a blender or food processor, combine frozen raspberries, water, and stevia.
- Blend until the mixture becomes smooth and creamy, scraping down the sides as needed.
- Transfer the sorbet mixture to a freezer-safe container and freeze for at least 3 hours or until firm.
- Once frozen, remove the sorbet from the freezer and let it sit at room temperature for a few minutes to soften slightly.
- Scoop the sorbet into bowls or glasses, garnish with fresh mint leaves, and serve immediately.
- Enjoy this refreshing and fruity dessert!

Nutritional Information:

- Calories: 50
- Carbohydrates: 12g
- Protein: 2g
- Fat: 1g
- Sodium: 0mg
- Potassium: 180mg
- Phosphorus: 40mg

## COCONUT FLOUR CHOCOLATE CHIP COOKIES WITH STEVIA

Time: 25 minutes

Servings: 12 cookies

Ingredients:

- 1/2 cup coconut flour
- 1/4 teaspoon baking soda
- 1/4 teaspoon salt
- 1/4 cup coconut oil, melted
- 2 tablespoons stevia (or sweetener of your choice)
- 2 large eggs
- 1 teaspoon vanilla extract
- 1/4 cup sugar-free dark chocolate chips

Directions:

- Preheat the oven to 350°F (175°C). Line a baking sheet with parchment paper.
- In a mixing bowl, whisk together coconut flour, baking soda, and salt.
- In a separate bowl, whisk together melted coconut oil, stevia, eggs, and vanilla extract until well combined.
- Add the wet ingredients to the dry ingredients and stir until a thick cookie dough forms.
- Fold in the sugar-free dark chocolate chips.
- Drop rounded tablespoons of dough onto the prepared baking sheet and flatten slightly with the back of a spoon.

- Bake in the preheated oven for 12-15 minutes or until the edges are golden brown.
- Remove from the oven and let the cookies cool on the baking sheet for 5 minutes, then transfer them to a wire rack to cool completely.
- Once cooled, the cookies are ready to be enjoyed. Store any leftovers in an airtight container.

Nutritional Information:

- Calories: 80
- Carbohydrates: 4g
- Protein: 2g
- Fat: 7g
- Sodium: 90mg
- Potassium: 30mg
- Phosphorus: 45mg

## SUGAR-FREE BLUEBERRY CRUMBLE WITH OAT TOPPING

Time: 45 minutes

Servings: 6

Ingredients:

*For the filling:*

- 4 cups fresh blueberries
- 2 tablespoons stevia (or sweetener of your choice)
- 1 tablespoon lemon juice
- 1 tablespoon cornstarch (optional, for thickening)

*For the oat topping:*

- 1 cup rolled oats
- 1/2 cup almond flour
- 1/4 cup chopped nuts (such as almonds or walnuts)
- 2 tablespoons melted coconut oil
- 2 tablespoons stevia (or sweetener of your choice)
- 1/2 teaspoon ground cinnamon

Directions:

- Preheat the oven to 375°F (190°C). Grease a baking dish.
- In a mixing bowl, combine fresh blueberries, stevia, lemon juice, and cornstarch (if using). Toss gently to coat the blueberries.
- Transfer the blueberry mixture to the greased baking dish, spreading it out evenly.
- In a separate bowl, combine rolled oats, almond flour, chopped nuts, melted coconut oil, stevia, and cinnamon. Mix well until the mixture resembles crumbles.
- Sprinkle the oat topping evenly over the blueberry filling.
- Bake in the preheated oven for 25-30 minutes or until the top is golden brown and the blueberry filling is bubbling.
- Remove from the oven and let the crumble cool for a few minutes before serving.
- Serve the sugar-free blueberry crumble warm as a delicious dessert, optionally topped with sugar-free whipped cream or vanilla Greek yogurt.

Nutritional Information:

- Calories: 180
- Carbohydrates: 20g
- Protein: 4g
- Fat: 9g
- Sodium: 40mg
- Potassium: 130mg
- Phosphorus: 90mg

## ALMOND FLOUR BROWNIES WITH UNSWEETENED APPLESAUCE

Time: 40 minutes

Servings: 9

Ingredients:

- 1 cup almond flour

- 1/4 cup unsweetened cocoa powder
- 1/4 teaspoon baking soda
- 1/4 teaspoon salt
- 1/4 cup unsweetened applesauce
- 1/4 cup coconut oil, melted
- 1/4 cup stevia (or sweetener of your choice)
- 2 large eggs
- 1 teaspoon vanilla extract
- 1/4 cup sugar-free dark chocolate chips (optional)

Directions:

- Preheat the oven to 350°F (175°C). Grease an 8x8-inch baking dish.
- In a mixing bowl, whisk together almond flour, cocoa powder, baking soda, and salt.
- In a separate bowl, whisk together unsweetened applesauce, melted coconut oil, stevia, eggs, and vanilla extract until well combined.
- Add the wet ingredients to the dry ingredients and stir until just combined.
- Fold in the sugar-free dark chocolate chips, if using.
- Pour the batter into the greased baking dish and spread it out evenly.
- Bake in the preheated oven for 20-25 minutes or until a toothpick inserted into the center comes out with a few moist crumbs.
- Remove from the oven and let the brownies cool completely in the baking dish before cutting into squares.
- Once cooled and cut, the almond flour brownies are ready to be enjoyed. Store any leftovers in an airtight container.

Nutritional Information:

- Calories: 120
- Carbohydrates: 5g

- Protein: 4g
- Fat: 10g
- Sodium: 90mg
- Potassium: 70mg
- Phosphorus: 65mg

## SUGAR-FREE PEACH COBBLER WITH ALMOND FLOUR BISCUITS

Time: 1 hour 15 minutes

Servings: 8

Ingredients:

*For the peach filling:*

- 4 cups sliced fresh peaches
- 2 tablespoons stevia (or sweetener of your choice)
- 1 tablespoon lemon juice
- 1 teaspoon ground cinnamon
- 1/4 teaspoon nutmeg (optional)
- 2 tablespoons cornstarch (optional, for thickening)

*For the almond flour biscuits:*

- 1 1/2 cups almond flour
- 1/4 cup coconut flour
- 2 tablespoons stevia (or sweetener of your choice)
- 2 teaspoons baking powder
- 1/4 teaspoon salt
- 1/4 cup unsalted butter, chilled and cubed
- 1/4 cup unsweetened almond milk
- 1 teaspoon vanilla extract

Directions:

- Preheat the oven to 375°F (190°C). Grease a baking dish.
- In a mixing bowl, combine sliced peaches, stevia, lemon juice, cinnamon, nutmeg (if using), and cornstarch (if using). Toss gently to coat the peaches.
- Transfer the peach mixture to the greased baking dish, spreading it out evenly.

- In a separate mixing bowl, whisk together almond flour, coconut flour, stevia, baking powder, and salt.
- Add the chilled and cubed butter to the flour mixture. Use a pastry cutter or your fingers to cut the butter into the flour until the mixture resembles coarse crumbs.
- In a small bowl, whisk together almond milk and vanilla extract.
- Gradually pour the almond milk mixture into the flour mixture, stirring until a dough forms.
- Drop spoonfuls of the biscuit dough onto the peaches, covering the filling evenly.
- Bake in the preheated oven for 30-35 minutes or until the biscuits are golden brown and the peach filling is bubbling.
- Remove from the oven and let the cobbler cool for a few minutes before serving.
- Serve the sugar-free peach cobbler warm as a delightful dessert, optionally topped with sugar-free whipped cream or vanilla Greek yogurt.

Nutritional Information:

- Calories: 200
- Carbohydrates: 10g
- Protein: 6g
- Fat: 16g
- Sodium: 140mg
- Potassium: 180mg
- Phosphorus: 95mg

## VANILLA CHIA PUDDING WITH FRESH FRUIT TOPPINGS

Time: 4 hours (including chilling time)

Servings: 4

Ingredients:

- 1/4 cup chia seeds
- 1 1/2 cups unsweetened almond milk
- 1 teaspoon vanilla extract
- 1 tablespoon stevia (or sweetener of your choice)
- Assorted fresh fruits for topping (such as berries, sliced bananas, or diced mango)

Directions:

- In a mixing bowl, combine chia seeds, almond milk, vanilla extract, and stevia. Stir well to combine.
- Cover the bowl and refrigerate for at least 4 hours or overnight, allowing the chia seeds to absorb the liquid and create a pudding-like consistency.
- Once chilled and set, give the chia pudding a good stir to break up any clumps.
- Divide the chia pudding into serving bowls or glasses.
- Top the pudding with your favorite fresh fruits.
- Serve the vanilla chia pudding with fresh fruit toppings chilled as a nutritious and satisfying dessert or even a breakfast option.

Nutritional Information:

- Calories: 90
- Carbohydrates: 7g
- Protein: 4g
- Fat: 6g
- Sodium: 90mg
- Potassium: 130mg
- Phosphorus: 90mg

## LEMON POPPY SEED MUFFINS WITH ALMOND FLOUR AND STEVIA

Time: 30 minutes

Servings: 12

Ingredients:

- 2 cups almond flour

- 1/4 cup coconut flour
- 1/4 cup stevia (or sweetener of your choice)
- 1 tablespoon poppy seeds
- 1 teaspoon baking powder
- 1/2 teaspoon baking soda
- 1/4 teaspoon salt
- 1/4 cup unsalted butter, melted
- 1/4 cup unsweetened almond milk
- 3 large eggs
- Zest of 1 lemon
- Juice of 1 lemon
- 1 teaspoon vanilla extract

Directions:

- Preheat the oven to 350°F (175°C). Line a muffin tin with paper liners.
- In a mixing bowl, whisk together almond flour, coconut flour, stevia, poppy seeds, baking powder, baking soda, and salt.
- In a separate bowl, whisk together melted butter, almond milk, eggs, lemon zest, lemon juice, and vanilla extract until well combined.
- Add the wet ingredients to the dry ingredients and stir until just combined, being careful not to overmix.
- Spoon the batter into the prepared muffin tin, filling each cup about 3/4 full.
- Bake in the preheated oven for 15-18 minutes or until a toothpick inserted into the center of a muffin comes out clean.
- Remove from the oven and let the muffins cool in the tin for 5 minutes, then transfer them to a wire rack to cool completely.
- Once cooled, the lemon poppy seed muffins are ready to be enjoyed. Store any leftovers in an airtight container.

Nutritional Information:

- Calories: 150
- Carbohydrates: 5g
- Protein: 6g
- Fat: 13g
- Sodium: 150mg
- Potassium: 60mg
- Phosphorus: 70mg

## MIXED BERRY FROZEN YOGURT WITH LOW-SUGAR GRANOLA

Time: 4 hours (including freezing time)

Servings: 4

Ingredients:

- 2 cups mixed berries (such as strawberries, blueberries, and raspberries), frozen
- 2 cups unsweetened Greek yogurt
- 1 tablespoon stevia (or sweetener of your choice)
- Low-sugar granola for topping

Directions:

- In a blender or food processor, combine frozen mixed berries, Greek yogurt, and stevia.
- Blend until the mixture becomes smooth and creamy, scraping down the sides as needed.
- Transfer the frozen yogurt mixture to a freezer-safe container and freeze for at least 4 hours or until firm.
- Once frozen, remove the frozen yogurt from the freezer and let it sit at room temperature for a few minutes to soften slightly.
- Scoop the frozen yogurt into bowls or glasses, sprinkle with low-sugar granola as a delicious topping.
- Serve the mixed berry frozen yogurt with low-sugar granola as a refreshing and guilt-free dessert.

Nutritional Information:

- Calories: 100
- Carbohydrates: 10g
- Protein: 8g
- Fat: 3g
- Sodium: 40mg
- Potassium: 250mg
- Phosphorus: 125mg

# BONUS CHAPTER: BEVERAGES AND REFRESHING DRINKS

## RECIPE: CUCUMBER MINT INFUSED WATER

Time: 5 minutes

Servings: 4

Ingredients:

- 1 large cucumber, sliced
- 10-12 fresh mint leaves
- 4 cups of water

Directions:

- In a pitcher, add the sliced cucumber and mint leaves.
- Pour water over the cucumber and mint.
- Stir gently to mix the ingredients.
- Refrigerate for at least 1 hour to allow the flavors to infuse.
- Serve chilled and enjoy the refreshing cucumber mint infused water.

Nutritional Information:

- Calories: 0
- Fat: 0g
- Carbohydrates: 0g
- Protein: 0g
- Sodium: 0mg
- Potassium: 0mg
- Phosphorus: 0mg
- Sugar: 0g

## RECIPE: FRESH LEMONADE (USING SUGAR SUBSTITUTES)

Time: 10 minutes

Servings: 4

Ingredients:

- 4 fresh lemons
- 4 cups of water
- Sugar substitute of your choice (according to taste)
- Ice cubes (optional)

Directions:

- Squeeze the juice from the lemons and strain it to remove any seeds or pulp.
- In a pitcher, combine the lemon juice, water, and desired amount of sugar substitute.
- Stir well until the sugar substitute dissolves.
- Add ice cubes if desired.
- Serve chilled and enjoy the refreshing sugar-free lemonade.

Nutritional Information:

- Calories: <5 (depending on the sugar substitute used)
- Fat: 0g
- Carbohydrates: <1g
- Protein: 0g
- Sodium: 0mg
- Potassium: <10mg (depending on the size of lemons used)
- Phosphorus: <10mg
- Sugar: 0g

## RECIPE: HIBISCUS ICED TEA (UNSWEETENED)

Time: 15 minutes

Servings: 4

Ingredients:

- 4 cups of water
- 4 hibiscus tea bags
- Ice cubes (optional)
- Lemon or lime wedges for garnish (optional)

Directions:

- Bring the water to a boil in a pot.

- Remove from heat and add the hibiscus tea bags.
- Steep for 5-7 minutes.
- Remove the tea bags and let the tea cool to room temperature.
- Once cooled, refrigerate until chilled.
- Serve over ice cubes if desired.
- Garnish with lemon or lime wedges if desired.
- Enjoy the refreshing unsweetened hibiscus iced tea.

Nutritional Information:

- Calories: 0
- Fat: 0g
- Carbohydrates: 0g
- Protein: 0g
- Sodium: 0mg
- Potassium: <10mg (depending on the strength of the tea)
- Phosphorus: <10mg
- Sugar: 0g

RECIPE: BERRY BLAST SMOOTHIE (MADE WITH LOW-POTASSIUM FRUITS LIKE BERRIES AND ALMOND MILK)

Time: 5 minutes

Servings: 2

Ingredients:

- 1 cup frozen mixed berries (such as strawberries, blueberries, and raspberries)
- 1 cup unsweetened almond milk
- 1 tablespoon sugar substitute (optional)
- Ice cubes (optional)

Directions:

- In a blender, combine the frozen mixed berries, almond milk, and sugar substitute (if desired).
- Blend until smooth and creamy.
- Add ice cubes if a colder consistency is desired.

- Pour into glasses and serve immediately.
- Enjoy the delicious and kidney-friendly berry blast smoothie.

Nutritional Information:

- Calories: <100 (depending on the specific fruits used)
- Fat: 3g (from almond milk)
- Carbohydrates: <10g (depending on the specific fruits used and sugar substitute)
- Protein: <5g
- Sodium: <100mg (depending on the almond milk)
- Potassium: <200mg (depending on the specific fruits used)
- Phosphorus: <100mg (depending on the almond milk)
- Sugar: <5g (depending on the specific fruits used and sugar substitute)

## RECIPE: GREEN TEA WITH LEMON (UNSWEETENED)

Time: 10 minutes

Servings: 2

Ingredients:

- 2 green tea bags
- 2 cups boiling water
- Fresh lemon slices for garnish (optional)

Directions:

- Place the green tea bags in a teapot or a heatproof container.
- Pour boiling water over the tea bags.
- Let the tea steep for 3-5 minutes.
- Remove the tea bags and let the tea cool to room temperature.
- Once cooled, refrigerate until chilled.
- Serve the unsweetened green tea over ice cubes if desired.

- Garnish with fresh lemon slices if desired.
- Enjoy the refreshing and antioxidant-rich green tea with lemon.

Nutritional Information:

- Calories: 0
- Fat: 0g
- Carbohydrates: 0g
- Protein: 0g
- Sodium: 0mg
- Potassium: <10mg (depending on the strength of the tea)
- Phosphorus: <10mg
- Sugar: 0g

## RECIPE: WATERMELON LIME SLUSHIE (USING SUGAR SUBSTITUTES)

Time: 10 minutes

Servings: 2

Ingredients:

- 2 cups of cubed seedless watermelon
- Juice of 1 lime
- Sugar substitute of your choice (according to taste)
- Ice cubes

Directions:

- Place the cubed watermelon in a blender.
- Squeeze the lime juice into the blender.
- Add the desired amount of sugar substitute.
- Blend until smooth.
- Add ice cubes and blend again until slushie consistency is achieved.
- Pour into glasses and serve immediately.
- Enjoy the refreshing watermelon lime slushie.

Nutritional Information:

- Calories: <50 (depending on the specific watermelon used and sugar substitute)
- Fat: 0g
- Carbohydrates: <10g
- Protein: <1g
- Sodium: 0mg
- Potassium: <100mg (depending on the specific watermelon used)
- Phosphorus: <10mg
- Sugar: <5g (depending on the specific watermelon used and sugar substitute)

## RECIPE: GINGER TURMERIC DETOX WATER

Time: 5 minutes

Servings: 4

Ingredients:

- 4 cups of water
- 1-inch piece of fresh ginger, sliced
- 1 teaspoon ground turmeric
- Juice of 1 lemon
- Ice cubes

Directions:

- In a pitcher, combine the water, sliced ginger, ground turmeric, and lemon juice.
- Stir well to mix the ingredients.
- Let the mixture sit for at least 10 minutes to allow the flavors to infuse.
- Add ice cubes to chill the detox water.
- Serve and enjoy the refreshing and detoxifying ginger turmeric water.

Nutritional Information:

- Calories: 0
- Fat: 0g
- Carbohydrates: <1g
- Protein: <1g
- Sodium: 0mg

- Potassium: <10mg (depending on the specific amount of ginger used)
- Phosphorus: <10mg
- Sugar: <1g (naturally occurring sugars from lemon)

## RECIPE: SPARKLING WATER WITH A SPLASH OF FRESH LIME JUICE

Time: 5 minutes

Servings: 2

Ingredients:

- 2 cups of sparkling water
- Juice of 1 lime
- Lime slices for garnish (optional)
- Ice cubes

Directions:

- In two glasses, divide the sparkling water equally.
- Squeeze the lime juice into the glasses, dividing it equally.
- Add ice cubes to each glass.
- Stir gently to mix the lime juice and sparkling water.
- Garnish with lime slices if desired.
- Serve the refreshing sparkling water with a splash of fresh lime juice.

Nutritional Information:

- Calories: <5
- Fat: 0g
- Carbohydrates: <1g
- Protein: 0g
- Sodium: 0mg
- Potassium: <10mg (depending on the specific amount of lime juice used)
- Phosphorus: 0mg
- Sugar: 0g

## RECIPE: ICED HERBAL TEA WITH STEVIA

Time: 15 minutes

Servings: 4

Ingredients:

- 4 cups of water
- 4 herbal tea bags of your choice (such as chamomile, mint, or rooibos)
- Stevia or other sugar substitute of your choice (according to taste)
- Ice cubes (optional)

Directions:

- Bring the water to a boil in a pot.
- Remove from heat and add the herbal tea bags.
- Steep for the recommended time according to the tea bag instructions.
- Remove the tea bags and let the tea cool to room temperature.
- Once cooled, refrigerate until chilled.
- Add stevia or your preferred sugar substitute to taste.
- Serve over ice cubes if desired.
- Enjoy the flavorful and sugar-free iced herbal tea.

Nutritional Information:

- Calories: <5
- Fat: 0g
- Carbohydrates: <1g
- Protein: 0g
- Sodium: 0mg
- Potassium: <10mg (depending on the specific herbal tea used)
- Phosphorus: <10mg
- Sugar: 0g

## RECIPE: COCONUT WATER (LOW IN POTASSIUM)

Time: N/A

Servings: 1

Ingredients:

- 1 cup of natural coconut water

Directions:

- Simply pour the desired amount of natural coconut water into a glass.
- Serve chilled and enjoy the refreshing and potassium-friendly coconut water.

Nutritional Information:

- Calories: 45 (may vary depending on the brand)
- Fat: 0g
- Carbohydrates: 11g
- Protein: 0g
- Sodium: 30mg
- Potassium: 470mg (may vary depending on the brand)
- Phosphorus: 48mg (may vary depending on the brand)
- Sugar: 9g (naturally occurring sugars)

## RECIPE: PINEAPPLE GINGER COOLER (USING SUGAR SUBSTITUTES)

Time: 10 minutes

Servings: 2

Ingredients:

- 1 cup pineapple chunks (fresh or canned in its juice)
- 1-inch piece of fresh ginger, peeled
- 1 cup of water
- Sugar substitute of your choice (according to taste)
- Ice cubes

Directions:

- In a blender, combine the pineapple chunks, fresh ginger, water, and desired amount of sugar substitute.
- Blend until smooth and well-combined.

- Strain the mixture if desired to remove any fibrous texture.
- Add ice cubes to glasses.
- Pour the pineapple ginger cooler over the ice cubes.
- Serve chilled and enjoy the tropical and sugar-free pineapple ginger cooler.

Nutritional Information:

- Calories: <50 (depending on the specific pineapple used and sugar substitute)
- Fat: 0g
- Carbohydrates: <10g
- Protein: <1g
- Sodium: <5mg
- Potassium: <100mg (depending on the specific pineapple used)
- Phosphorus: <10mg
- Sugar: <5g (depending on the specific pineapple used and sugar substitute)

## RECIPE: UNSWEETENED ALMOND MILK LATTE

Time: 10 minutes

Servings: 1

Ingredients:

- 1 cup unsweetened almond milk
- 1 shot of espresso or 1/2 cup of strong brewed coffee
- Cinnamon or nutmeg for sprinkling (optional)

Directions:

- Heat the almond milk in a small saucepan over medium heat until hot but not boiling.
- Froth the heated almond milk using a frother or whisk until foamy.
- Brew a shot of espresso or prepare strong brewed coffee.
- Pour the espresso or coffee into a mug.

- Gently pour the frothed almond milk over the espresso or coffee, holding back the foam with a spoon.
- Spoon the remaining foam on top of the latte.
- Sprinkle with cinnamon or nutmeg if desired.
- Enjoy the creamy and dairy-free unsweetened almond milk latte.

Nutritional Information:

- Calories: <30
- Fat: 2.5g
- Carbohydrates: <1g
- Protein: <1g
- Sodium: <5mg
- Potassium: <50mg
- Phosphorus: <10mg
- Sugar: 0g

## RECIPE: CRANBERRY SPRITZER (USING UNSWEETENED CRANBERRY JUICE)

Time: 5 minutes

Servings: 2

Ingredients:

- 1/2 cup unsweetened cranberry juice
- 1 1/2 cups sparkling water
- Juice of 1 lime
- Stevia or other sugar substitute of your choice (according to taste)
- Ice cubes
- Fresh cranberries for garnish (optional)

Directions:

- In a pitcher, combine the unsweetened cranberry juice, sparkling water, lime juice, and desired amount of sugar substitute.
- Stir well to mix the ingredients.
- Add ice cubes to glasses.

- Pour the cranberry spritzer over the ice cubes.
- Garnish with fresh cranberries if desired.
- Serve chilled and enjoy the tangy and sugar-free cranberry spritzer.

Nutritional Information:

- Calories: <20
- Fat: 0g
- Carbohydrates: <5g
- Protein: 0g
- Sodium: <5mg
- Potassium: <10mg
- Phosphorus: <10mg
- Sugar: 0g

### RECIPE: PEPPERMINT ICED MOCHA (USING SUGAR SUBSTITUTES AND UNSWEETENED COCOA)

Time: 10 minutes

Servings: 2

Ingredients:

- 2 cups of unsweetened almond milk
- 1 shot of espresso or 1/2 cup of strong brewed coffee
- 2 tablespoons unsweetened cocoa powder
- Peppermint extract to taste
- Sugar substitute of your choice (according to taste)
- Ice cubes
- Whipped cream for topping (optional)

Directions:

- In a small saucepan, heat the almond milk over medium heat until hot but not boiling.
- Whisk in the unsweetened cocoa powder until well combined and smooth.
- Stir in the espresso or coffee, peppermint extract, and desired amount of sugar substitute.

- Remove from heat and let the mixture cool to room temperature.
- Once cooled, refrigerate until chilled.
- Add ice cubes to glasses.
- Pour the peppermint iced mocha over the ice cubes.
- Top with whipped cream if desired.
- Serve chilled and enjoy the rich and refreshing peppermint iced mocha.

Nutritional Information:

- Calories: <50
- Fat: 2.5g
- Carbohydrates: <5g
- Protein: <1g
- Sodium: <5mg
- Potassium: <50mg
- Phosphorus: <10mg
- Sugar: <1g (depending on the specific sugar substitute used)

## RECIPE: HERBAL ICED TEA BLEND (USING KIDNEY-SAFE HERBS LIKE CHAMOMILE AND ROOIBOS)

Time: 10 minutes

Servings: 4

Ingredients:

- 4 cups of water
- 4 herbal tea bags (chamomile, rooibos, or a blend of kidney-safe herbs)
- Stevia or other sugar substitute of your choice (according to taste)
- Lemon slices for garnish (optional)
- Ice cubes

Directions:

- Bring the water to a boil in a pot.
- Remove from heat and add the herbal tea bags.

- Steep for the recommended time according to the tea bag instructions.
- Remove the tea bags and let the tea cool to room temperature.
- Once cooled, refrigerate until chilled.
- Add stevia or your preferred sugar substitute to taste.
- Serve over ice cubes.
- Garnish with lemon slices if desired.
- Enjoy the refreshing and kidney-friendly herbal iced tea blend.

Nutritional Information:

- Calories: <5
- Fat: 0g
- Carbohydrates: <1g
- Protein: 0g
- Sodium: <5mg
- Potassium: <10mg (depending on the specific herbal tea blend used)
- Phosphorus: <10mg
- Sugar: 0g

## RECIPE: SPARKLING CUCUMBER LIMEADE

Time: 10 minutes

Servings: 2

Ingredients:

- 1 cucumber, peeled and sliced
- Juice of 2 limes
- 2 cups of sparkling water
- Stevia or other sugar substitute of your choice (according to taste)
- Fresh mint leaves for garnish (optional)
- Ice cubes

Directions:

- In a blender, combine the sliced cucumber and lime juice.
- Blend until smooth.
- Strain the mixture to remove any pulp.

- In a pitcher, combine the cucumber-lime mixture, sparkling water, and desired amount of sugar substitute.
- Stir well to mix the ingredients.
- Add ice cubes to glasses.
- Pour the sparkling cucumber limeade over the ice cubes.
- Garnish with fresh mint leaves if desired.
- Serve chilled and enjoy the fizzy and refreshing cucumber limeade.

Nutritional Information:

- Calories: <20
- Fat: 0g
- Carbohydrates: <5g
- Protein: 0g
- Sodium: <5mg
- Potassium: <50mg (depending on the specific cucumber used)
- Phosphorus: <10mg
- Sugar: <1g (depending on the specific sugar substitute used)

RECIPE: MINTY FRESH GREEN SMOOTHIE (MADE WITH LOW-POTASSIUM GREENS LIKE SPINACH)

Time: 5 minutes

Servings: 1

Ingredients:

- 1 cup unsweetened almond milk
- 1 cup fresh baby spinach leaves
- 1/2 ripe avocado
- 1/4 cup fresh mint leaves
- Stevia or other sugar substitute of your choice (according to taste)
- Ice cubes

Directions:

- In a blender, combine the unsweetened almond milk, spinach leaves, avocado, mint leaves, and desired amount of sugar substitute.
- Blend until smooth and creamy.

- Add ice cubes and blend again until well incorporated.
- Pour the minty fresh green smoothie into a glass.
- Serve chilled and enjoy the nutritious and kidney-friendly smoothie.

Nutritional Information:

- Calories: <150
- Fat: 10g
- Carbohydrates: <10g
- Protein: <5g
- Sodium: <5mg
- Potassium: <200mg (depending on the specific spinach used)
- Phosphorus: <50mg
- Sugar: <1g (depending on the specific sugar substitute used)

## RECIPE: BLUEBERRY BASIL LEMONADE (USING SUGAR SUBSTITUTES)

Time: 15 minutes

Servings: 2

Ingredients:

- 1 cup fresh blueberries
- 1/4 cup fresh basil leaves
- Juice of 2 lemons
- Stevia or other sugar substitute of your choice (according to taste)
- 2 cups of water
- Ice cubes
- Fresh blueberries and basil leaves for garnish (optional)

Directions:

- In a blender, combine the fresh blueberries, basil leaves, lemon juice, desired amount of sugar substitute, and water.
- Blend until smooth and well combined.
- Strain the mixture to remove any pulp or seeds.
- Add ice cubes to glasses.

- Pour the blueberry basil lemonade over the ice cubes.
- Garnish with fresh blueberries and basil leaves if desired.
- Serve chilled and enjoy the tangy and sugar-free blueberry basil lemonade.

Nutritional Information:

- Calories: <50
- Fat: 0g
- Carbohydrates: <10g
- Protein: <1g
- Sodium: <5mg
- Potassium: <50mg (depending on the specific blueberries used)
- Phosphorus: <10mg
- Sugar: <1g (depending on the specific sugar substitute used)

## RECIPE: WATER WITH A TWIST OF FRESH CITRUS (ORANGE, GRAPEFRUIT, OR LIME)

Time: N/A

Servings: 1

Ingredients:

- 1 cup of water
- Slices of fresh citrus fruits (orange, grapefruit, or lime)

Directions:

- Fill a glass with water.
- Add slices of fresh citrus fruits to the water.
- Stir gently to infuse the flavors.
- Serve chilled and enjoy the simple and hydrating water with a twist of fresh citrus.

Nutritional Information:

- Calories: <5
- Fat: 0g
- Carbohydrates: <1g
- Protein: 0g

- Sodium: <5mg
- Potassium: <10mg (depending on the specific citrus fruit used)
- Phosphorus: <10mg
- Sugar: <1g (naturally occurring sugars from the citrus fruit)

## RECIPE: ICED DECAF COFFEE WITH SUGAR-FREE SYRUP

Time: 5 minutes

Servings: 1

Ingredients:

- 1 cup of decaffeinated coffee, brewed and chilled
- Sugar-free syrup of your choice (according to taste)
- Ice cubes
- Unsweetened almond milk (optional)

Directions:

- Brew a cup of decaffeinated coffee and let it cool to room temperature.
- Pour the chilled coffee into a glass.
- Add the desired amount of sugar-free syrup and stir well.
- Add ice cubes to the glass.
- If desired, add a splash of unsweetened almond milk.
- Stir again to combine all the ingredients.
- Serve chilled and enjoy the refreshing and caffeine-free iced coffee.

Nutritional Information:

- Calories: <10
- Fat: 0g
- Carbohydrates: <1g
- Protein: <1g
- Sodium: <5mg
- Potassium: <50mg (depending on the specific decaffeinated coffee used)
- Phosphorus: <10mg
- Sugar: 0g

# 30-DAY DIABETIC RENAL MEAL PLAN

## DAY 1:

Breakfast: Vegetable Egg Scramble with Spinach and Mushrooms

Lunch: Lentil Soup with Carrots and Celery

Dinner: Baked Salmon with Dill and Lemon

Snack: Greek Yogurt Parfait with Low-Sugar Granola and Chopped Nuts

## DAY 2:

Breakfast: Oatmeal with Fresh Berries and Cinnamon

Lunch: Greek Salad with Feta Cheese and Olives (low-sodium version)

Dinner: Quinoa-Stuffed Bell Peppers with Ground Turkey and Low-Sodium Seasoning

Snack: Chia Seed Pudding with Unsweetened Coconut Flakes

## DAY 3:

Breakfast: Whole Wheat Pancakes with Sugar-Free Fruit Compote

Lunch: Tomato and Basil Soup with Low-Sodium Broth

Dinner: Grilled Chicken Breast with Herbs and Spices

Snack: Cottage Cheese with Sliced Peaches and Flaxseed

## DAY 4:

Breakfast: Quinoa Breakfast Bowl with Almond Milk and Sliced Almonds

Lunch: Cucumber and Avocado Salad with Lemon Vinaigrette

Dinner: Shrimp Stir-Fry with Low-Sodium Soy Sauce and Vegetables

Snack: Avocado and Tomato Toast on Whole Grain Bread

## DAY 5:

Breakfast: Egg White Omelette with Low-Potassium Vegetables

Lunch: Lentil Curry with Brown Rice and Spinach

Dinner: Turkey Chili with Kidney Beans and Low-Sodium Seasoning

Snack: Buckwheat Pancakes with Sugar-Free Maple Syrup

## DAY 6:

Breakfast: Chia Seed Pudding with Unsweetened Cocoa Powder and Fresh Berries

Lunch: Spinach Salad with Strawberries and Balsamic Dressing (low-sugar version)

Dinner: Baked Tofu with Low-Sodium Teriyaki Sauce and Brown Rice

Snack: Smoothie Bowl with Spinach, Almond Milk, and Berries

## DAY 7:

Breakfast: Low-Sodium Breakfast Casserole with Turkey Sausage and Bell Peppers

Lunch: Bean and Vegetable Minestrone Soup (low-sodium version)

Dinner: Lemon Herb Grilled Chicken Thighs with Steamed Broccoli

Snack: Almond Flour Banana Muffins with Stevia

## DAY 8:

Breakfast: Sweet Potato Hash Browns with Low-Sodium Seasoning

Lunch: Quinoa Salad with Roasted Vegetables and Lemon Dressing

Dinner: Grilled Vegetable Skewers with Balsamic Glaze

Snack: Sugar-Free Lemon Bars with Almond Flour Crust

## DAY 9:

Breakfast: Ricotta and Berry Stuffed French Toast with Whole Grain Bread

Lunch: Broccoli and Cheddar Soup with Low-Sodium Stock

Dinner: Baked Cod with Herbed Quinoa Pilaf

Snack: Greek Yogurt Bark with Sugar-Free Dark Chocolate and Nuts

## DAY 10:

Breakfast: Veggie Frittata with Zucchini, Bell Peppers, and Onion

Lunch: Mixed Green Salad with Grilled Chicken and Low-Phosphorus Dressing

Dinner: Grilled Steak with Mushroom Sauce and Steamed Asparagus

Snack: Pumpkin Spice Muffins with Almond Flour and Stevia

## DAY 11:

Breakfast: Breakfast Quinoa with Sliced Apples and Cinnamon

Lunch: Butternut Squash Soup with Cinnamon and Nutmeg

Dinner: Lentil Soup with Carrots and Celery

Snack: Raspberry Sorbet with Fresh Mint Leaves

## DAY 12:

Breakfast: Low-Sugar Bran Muffins with Walnuts

Lunch: Asian Chicken Salad with Ginger-Sesame Dressing (low-sodium version)

Dinner: Spinach Salad with Strawberries and Balsamic Dressing (low-sugar version)

Snack: Coconut Flour Chocolate Chip Cookies with Stevia

## DAY 13:

Breakfast: Veggie Breakfast Wrap with Egg Whites and Low-Sodium Cheese

Lunch: Cauliflower and Leek Soup with Low-Sodium Seasoning

Dinner: Chicken and Vegetable Soup with Herbs and Spices

Snack: Sugar-Free Blueberry Crumble with Oat Topping

## DAY 14:

Breakfast: Tomato and Basil Soup with Low-Sodium Broth

Lunch: Greek Salad with Feta Cheese and Olives (low-sodium version)

Dinner: Quinoa-Stuffed Bell Peppers with Ground Turkey and Low-Sodium Seasoning

Snack: Almond Flour Brownies with Unsweetened Applesauce

## DAY 15:

Breakfast: Lemon Poppy Seed Muffins with Almond Flour and Stevia

Lunch: Lentil Curry with Brown Rice and Spinach

Dinner: Shrimp Stir-Fry with Low-Sodium Soy Sauce and Vegetables

Snack: Mixed Berry Frozen Yogurt with Low-Sugar Granola

## DAY 16:

Breakfast: Baked Apples with Cinnamon and Greek Yogurt

Lunch: Cucumber and Avocado Salad with Lemon Vinaigrette

Dinner: Baked Chicken with Roasted Brussels Sprouts and Sweet Potatoes

Snack: Sugar-Free Cheesecake with Almond Flour Crust

## DAY 17:

Breakfast: Mixed Berry Frozen Yogurt with Low-Sugar Granola

Lunch: Quinoa Salad with Roasted Vegetables and Lemon Dressing

Dinner: Grilled Vegetable Skewers with Balsamic Glaze

Snack: Vanilla Chia Pudding with Fresh Fruit Toppings

## DAY 18:

Breakfast: Oatmeal with Fresh Berries and Cinnamon

Lunch: Lentil Soup with Carrots and Celery

Dinner: Baked Salmon with Dill and Lemon

Snack: Chocolate Avocado Mousse with Stevia

## DAY 19:

Breakfast: Greek Yogurt Parfait with Low-Sugar Granola and Chopped Nuts

Lunch: Tomato and Basil Soup with Low-Sodium Broth

Dinner: Grilled Chicken Breast with Herbs and Spices

Snack: Sugar-Free Lemon Bars with Almond Flour Crust

## DAY 20:

Breakfast: Quinoa Breakfast Bowl with Almond Milk and Sliced Almonds

Lunch: Cucumber and Avocado Salad with Lemon Vinaigrette

Dinner: Shrimp Stir-Fry with Low-Sodium Soy Sauce and Vegetables

Snack: Chia Seed Pudding with Unsweetened Coconut Flakes

## DAY 21:

Breakfast: Buckwheat Pancakes with Sugar-Free Maple Syrup

Lunch: Lentil Curry with Brown Rice and Spinach

Dinner: Turkey Chili with Kidney Beans and Low-Sodium Seasoning

Snack: Greek Yogurt Bark with Sugar-Free Dark Chocolate and Nuts

## DAY 22:

Breakfast: Egg White Omelette with Low-Potassium Vegetables

Lunch: Lentil Soup with Carrots and Celery

Dinner: Baked Tofu with Low-Sodium Teriyaki Sauce and Brown Rice

Snack: Pumpkin Spice Muffins with Almond Flour and Stevia

## DAY 23:

Breakfast: Chia Seed Pudding with Unsweetened Cocoa Powder and Fresh Berries

Lunch: Spinach Salad with Strawberries and Balsamic Dressing (low-sugar version)

Dinner: Grilled Chicken Breast with Herbs and Spices

Snack: Coconut Flour Chocolate Chip Cookies with Stevia

## DAY 24:

Breakfast: Low-Sodium Breakfast Casserole with Turkey Sausage and Bell Peppers

Lunch: Bean and Vegetable Minestrone Soup (low-sodium version)

Dinner: Lemon Herb Grilled Chicken Thighs with Steamed Broccoli

Snack: Almond Flour Banana Muffins with Stevia

## DAY 25:

Breakfast: Sweet Potato Hash Browns with Low-Sodium Seasoning

Lunch: Quinoa Salad with Roasted Vegetables and Lemon Dressing

Dinner: Grilled Vegetable Skewers with Balsamic Glaze

Snack: Sugar-Free Lemon Bars with Almond Flour Crust

## DAY 26:

Breakfast: Ricotta and Berry Stuffed French Toast with Whole Grain Bread

Lunch: Broccoli and Cheddar Soup with Low-Sodium Stock

Dinner: Baked Cod with Herbed Quinoa Pilaf

Snack: Greek Yogurt Bark with Sugar-Free Dark Chocolate and Nuts

## DAY 27:

Breakfast: Veggie Frittata with Zucchini, Bell Peppers, and Onion

Lunch: Mixed Green Salad with Grilled Chicken and Low-Phosphorus Dressing

Dinner: Grilled Steak with Mushroom Sauce and Steamed Asparagus

Snack: Pumpkin Spice Muffins with Almond Flour and Stevia

## DAY 28:

Breakfast: Breakfast Quinoa with Sliced Apples and Cinnamon

Lunch: Tomato and Basil Soup with Low-Sodium Broth

Dinner: Quinoa-Stuffed Bell Peppers with Ground Turkey and Low-Sodium Seasoning

Snack: Almond Flour Brownies with Unsweetened Applesauce

## DAY 29:

Breakfast: Lemon Poppy Seed Muffins with Almond Flour and Stevia

Lunch: Lentil Curry with Brown Rice and Spinach

Dinner: Shrimp Stir-Fry with Low-Sodium Soy Sauce and Vegetables

Snack: Mixed Berry Frozen Yogurt with Low-Sugar Granola

## DAY 30:

Breakfast: Baked Apples with Cinnamon and Greek Yogurt

Lunch: Cucumber and Avocado Salad with Lemon Vinaigrette

Dinner: Baked Chicken with Roasted Brussels Sprouts and Sweet Potatoes

Snack: Sugar-Free Cheesecake with Almond Flour Crust

Remember to drink plenty of water throughout the day and adjust portion sizes as necessary. It's always a good idea to consult with a healthcare professional or registered dietitian for personalized advice and modifications to the meal plan based on your specific dietary needs and preferences.

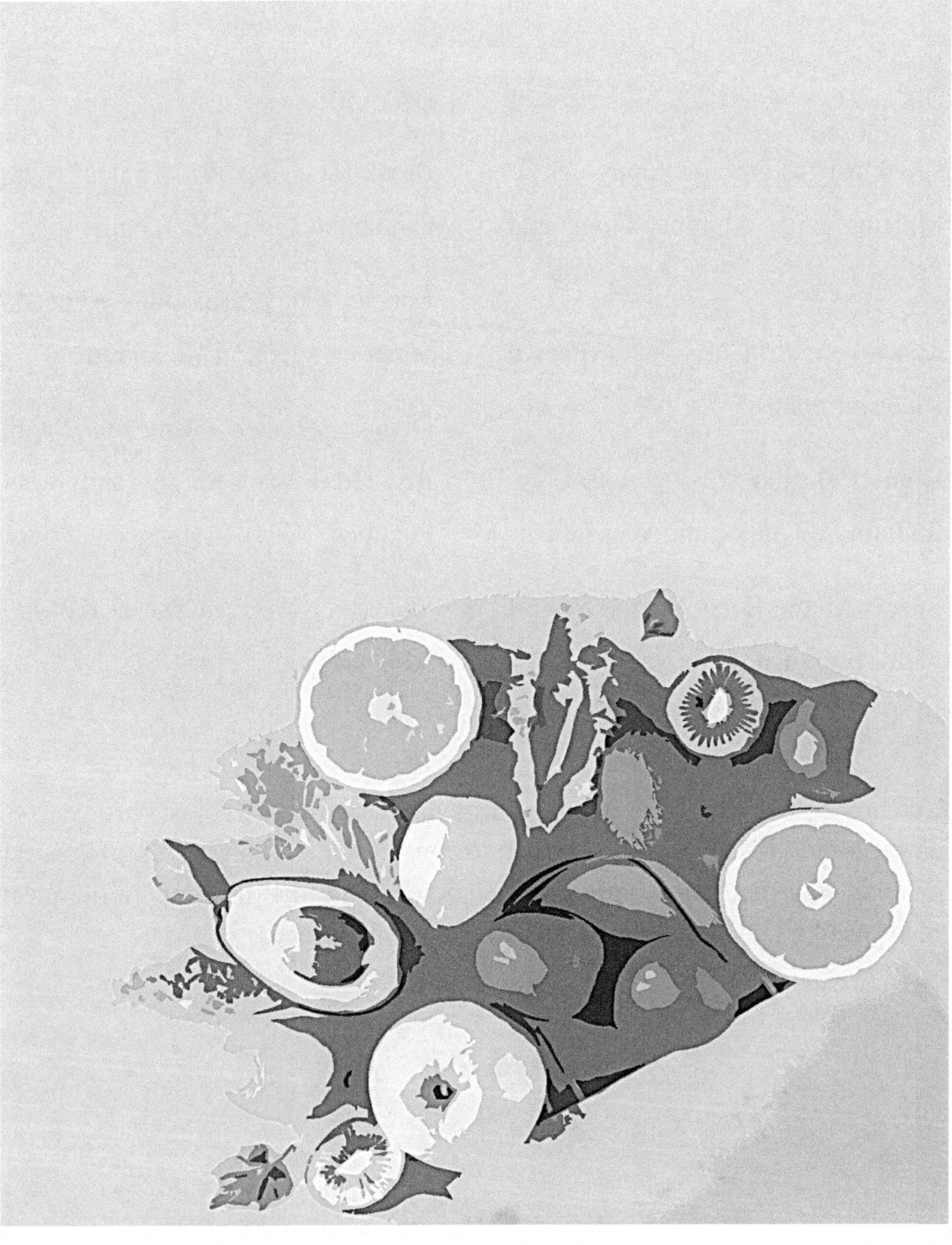

# CHAPTER 13: DINING OUT AND SPECIAL OCCASIONS

Dining out and special occasions often bring excitement and anticipation, but for individuals with diabetes and renal disease, they can also present unique challenges. This chapter aims to provide you with practical strategies and insights to navigate restaurant menus, make informed choices while dining out, and modify recipes to suit special occasions while still prioritizing your health. By empowering you with knowledge and tips, we hope to ensure that you can enjoy these moments without compromising your dietary goals and overall well-being.

## NAVIGATING RESTAURANT MENUS

When dining out, it's important to approach the restaurant menu with a mindful and informed mindset. Here are some strategies to help you make healthier choices:

- Familiarize Yourself with the Menu: Take time to review the menu before visiting the restaurant. Look for keywords that indicate healthier options, such as "grilled," "baked," "steamed," or "roasted." These cooking methods tend to use less added fats and oils compared to fried or breaded dishes.

- Opt for Lean Protein: Choose lean sources of protein, such as skinless poultry, fish, or legumes. These options are lower in saturated fats and can help maintain stable blood sugar levels.

- Load Up on Vegetables: Make vegetables the star of your meal. Look for salads, steamed vegetables, or vegetable-based dishes. They provide essential nutrients, dietary fiber, and are generally low in carbohydrates.

- Be Mindful of Portion Sizes: Restaurant portions are often larger than what is necessary. Consider sharing a meal or ask for a take-out container to portion out a suitable amount before you start eating. This helps you avoid overeating and manage your blood sugar levels effectively.

## TIPS FOR EATING OUT WITH DIABETES AND RENAL DISEASE

For individuals managing both diabetes and renal disease, it's crucial to pay attention to sodium, phosphorus, and potassium content in restaurant meals. Here are some tips to keep in mind:

- Limit Sodium Intake: Ask the restaurant to prepare your meal with reduced sodium or no added salt. Avoid high-sodium condiments, such as soy sauce or salad dressings, and opt for low-sodium alternatives when available.

- Control Phosphorus Intake: Limit foods high in phosphorus, such as dairy products, nuts, and processed meats. Request substitutions or modifications to reduce phosphorus content in dishes, such as opting for non-dairy alternatives or choosing lean cuts of meat.

- Manage Potassium Levels: Foods rich in potassium, like bananas, tomatoes, and potatoes, may need to be limited for individuals with compromised kidney function. Communicate your dietary restrictions to the restaurant staff and ask for suitable alternatives or modifications.
- Stay Hydrated: Drinking plenty of water is essential for kidney health. Opt for water or unsweetened beverages instead of sugary or high-sodium options like soda or sports drinks.

## MODIFYING RECIPES FOR SPECIAL OCCASIONS

Special occasions call for celebration, and with a few modifications, you can still enjoy the festivities while maintaining a diabetic and renal-friendly diet. Here are some ideas to modify recipes:

- Reduce Added Sugars: When preparing sweet treats, reduce the amount of added sugars by using natural sweeteners like stevia, monk fruit, or sugar-free alternatives. Increase the use of flavorful spices, like cinnamon or nutmeg, to enhance the sweetness without adding extra sugar.
- Choose Whole Grains: Substitute refined grains with whole grains in recipes to increase fiber content and promote stable blood sugar levels. Incorporate whole wheat flour, quinoa, or brown rice into baked goods, side dishes, or stuffing recipes.
- Modify Sauces and Dressings: Opt for homemade sauces and dressings using low-sodium ingredients. Replace heavy cream or butter-based sauces

with lighter alternatives, such as yogurt or Greek yogurt, to reduce saturated fat content.

- Balance Flavors: Experiment with herbs, spices, and citrus juices to add depth and flavor to your dishes. This can help reduce the need for excess salt or high-sodium seasonings.

Dining out and special occasions don't have to be stressful or derail your dietary goals. By navigating restaurant menus with mindfulness, understanding the impact of sodium, phosphorus, and potassium on renal health, and modifying recipes to suit your needs, you can enjoy these occasions while prioritizing your health. Remember, knowledge and preparation are key to making informed choices, and with the right strategies, you can savor special moments without compromising your well-being.

# CHAPTER 14: LIFESTYLE TIPS FOR DIABETES AND KIDNEY HEALTH

Maintaining a healthy lifestyle is crucial for individuals with diabetes, especially when it comes to kidney health. Diabetes is a leading cause of kidney disease, also known as diabetic nephropathy, which can lead to kidney failure if left untreated. In this chapter, we will explore lifestyle tips that focus on regular physical activity, stress management techniques, and monitoring both blood sugar and kidney function to promote overall well-being and prevent complications.

## REGULAR PHYSICAL ACTIVITY AND ITS BENEFITS

Engaging in regular physical activity is not only beneficial for managing diabetes but also plays a vital role in promoting kidney health. Exercise helps to control blood sugar levels, improve insulin sensitivity, and reduce the risk of cardiovascular complications. Scientific studies have shown that regular physical activity can also have positive effects on kidney function.

- Control Blood Sugar Levels: Physical activity helps to lower blood sugar levels by increasing insulin sensitivity and improving glucose uptake by the muscles. This reduces the strain on the kidneys, as they have to filter less glucose from the bloodstream.

- Improve Blood Pressure: High blood pressure, also known as hypertension, is a common complication of diabetes that can lead to kidney damage. Regular exercise has been shown to lower blood pressure, reducing the risk of kidney problems.

- Enhance Circulation: Exercise improves blood flow and circulation throughout the body, including the kidneys. This promotes efficient filtration and waste removal, supporting optimal kidney function.

- Weight Management: Maintaining a healthy weight is important for kidney health. Regular physical activity helps to manage weight by burning calories, reducing body fat, and increasing muscle mass, all of which contribute to improved kidney function. To incorporate physical activity into your daily routine, consider activities such as brisk walking, cycling, swimming, or aerobic exercises. Aim for at least 150 minutes of moderate-intensity aerobic activity per week, along with strength training exercises two or more days a week to improve muscle strength.

## STRESS MANAGEMENT TECHNIQUES

Chronic stress can have detrimental effects on both diabetes management and kidney health. When we experience stress, our bodies release stress hormones such as cortisol, which can increase blood sugar levels and blood pressure, putting additional strain on the kidneys. Implementing stress management techniques can help reduce these effects and improve overall well-being.

- Mindfulness Meditation: Mindfulness meditation involves focusing your attention on the present moment, bringing awareness to your thoughts and emotions without judgment. Studies have shown that regular practice of mindfulness meditation can reduce stress, improve emotional well-being, and enhance kidney function.

- Deep Breathing Exercises: Deep breathing exercises, such as diaphragmatic breathing or belly breathing, can activate the body's relaxation response, counteracting the physiological effects of stress. These exercises promote relaxation, reduce anxiety, and help regulate blood pressure.

- Engage in Relaxation Techniques: Explore relaxation techniques such as progressive muscle relaxation, guided imagery, or yoga. These practices can help release tension, promote relaxation, and reduce stress levels.

- Engage in Hobbies and Activities: Engaging in activities that you enjoy and that promote relaxation can significantly reduce stress. Whether it's reading, listening to music, gardening, or spending time with loved ones, finding activities that bring you joy can help alleviate stress and improve overall well-being.

## MONITORING BLOOD SUGAR AND KIDNEY FUNCTION

Regular monitoring of blood sugar levels and kidney function is essential for individuals with diabetes and those at risk for kidney disease. By closely monitoring these parameters, you can identify any potential issues early on and take necessary steps to prevent complications. Here are some monitoring techniques to consider:

- Self-Monitoring of Blood Glucose (SMBG): Regularly checking your blood sugar levels using a glucometer allows you to track fluctuations and make necessary adjustments to your diabetes management plan. Consistently maintaining target blood glucose levels can help protect kidney function.
- Hemoglobin A1c (HbA1c) Testing: HbA1c testing provides a long-term measure of blood sugar control over the past two to three months. This test reflects average blood sugar levels and is an essential tool in assessing overall diabetes management.
- Kidney Function Tests: Monitoring kidney function involves tests such as measuring creatinine levels, estimated glomerular filtration rate (eGFR), and urine albumin-to-creatinine ratio (UACR). These tests help evaluate kidney health and detect any signs of kidney damage or dysfunction.
- Regular Medical Check-ups: Regular visits to your healthcare provider are crucial for monitoring both diabetes and kidney health. They can provide valuable insights, guidance, and necessary adjustments to your treatment plan.

Remember, always consult with your healthcare provider for personalized advice and recommendations regarding monitoring blood sugar and kidney function.

By incorporating regular physical activity, practicing stress management techniques, and monitoring blood sugar and kidney function, you can proactively protect your kidneys and overall health while managing diabetes. Taking these lifestyle tips to heart will not only benefit your well-being today but also contribute to a healthier and more fulfilling future. Stay committed, stay informed, and prioritize your health every step of the way.

# RECOMMENDED READING

Dear Readers,

I am thrilled to introduce you to a talented medical colleague of mine and fellow cookbook author, Aubrette LaGarde. She is also one of my closest friends, haha. Aubrette's passion for health, food, and her dedication to creating delicious recipes have always inspired me, and I am delighted to have the opportunity to feature three of her exceptional diet cookbooks in this edition.

I and Aubrette go way back, and I have been a fan of her culinary creations. Her innovative approach to flavors, meticulous attention to detail, and unwavering commitment to quality shine through in every dish. I am confident that you will find that her recipes are targeted to maximize health and delicious, and I wholeheartedly recommend exploring her cookbooks to elevate your culinary adventures.

To further support Aubrette, I have included three pictures of her related diet cookbooks below along with a direct link to purchase it on Amazon. I have also included a **QR CODE** that directs you to her author page on Amazon once scanned with your smartphone. That way, you get to explore the other amazing cookbook options she has to offer as well.

KIDNEY DISEASE DIET COOKBOOK FOR STAGE 3 BY AUBRETTE LAGARDE. AVAILABLE ON AMAZON. CLICK LINK TO GET A COPY.

(Paperback)

(Kindle)

KIDNEY DISEASE FOOD CHART BY AUBRETTE LAGARDE. AVAILABLE ON AMAZON. CLICK LINK TO GET A COPY.

(Paperback)

(Kindle)

DIABETIC RENAL DIET COOKBOOK FOR SENIORS BY AUBRETTE LAGARDE. AVAILABLE ON AMAZON. CLICK LINK TO GET A COPY.

(Paperback)

(Kindle)

SCAN QR CODE WITH
PHONE CAMERA OR SCANNER
APP TO SEE MORE OF OUR
COOKBOOKS ON AMAZON

OR CLICK HERE

I want to assure you that my intention in featuring Aubrette's cookbook(s) is purely to celebrate her talent, dedication to caring for the health of others, and contribute to the culinary community. There is no intention to mislead or confuse, compete or self-promote; rather, it is a gesture of support and camaraderie among colleagues who share a passion for good food, great cooking, and sustainable wellbeing of others.

I would also like to extend my heartfelt gratitude to Aubrette LaGarde for graciously allowing me to feature her cookbook in this edition. Aubrette, your culinary prowess is an inspiration to us all, and I am honored to showcase your work alongside mine.

Thank you, dear readers, for joining me on this culinary adventure, and I hope you enjoy exploring Aubrette's cookbooks and recipes as much as I have.

Warm regards,

Hermione Mendez.

# CONCLUSION

As I reach the conclusion of this cookbook, a sense of fulfillment and optimism washes over me. I am confident that the recipes and tips shared throughout these pages will greatly assist individuals dealing with diabetes and renal issues in leading healthier and more content lives. Moreover, I hold a belief that through making small adjustments to our diet and lifestyle, we can seize control of our well-being and overall health.

Living with diabetes and renal challenges may seem daunting, yet it is vital to recognize that we are not alone in this journey. With the support of our loved ones and healthcare professionals, we can navigate the obstacles that arise and implement positive transformations that will nurture both our bodies and minds.

This cookbook is far more than a mere compilation of recipes; it serves as a valuable tool in empowering us to take charge of our health. By adhering to the guidelines and suggestions provided, we can learn to prepare delectable and nourishing meals that effectively regulate our blood sugar levels while also supporting our renal health.

Nevertheless, this cookbook also serves as a gentle reminder that we all possess the capacity to bring about positive changes in our lives. Whether it entails mastering a new recipe, engaging in a daily walk, or simply taking a moment to practice deep breathing and centering ourselves, we each hold the power to take small but significant steps towards a healthier and more content future.

As you conclude your perusal of this book, remember that you possess tremendous potential for personal growth. You hold the authority to initiate positive changes within your life, beginning with the food choices you make. Embrace the journey that lies ahead, and may your path be adorned with a sense of fulfillment, optimism, and delightful meals that contribute to your overall well-being.

# APPENDIX

In the pursuit of optimal health, it is essential to address specific dietary considerations for individuals managing both diabetes and renal (kidney) conditions. This comprehensive appendix provides valuable information on how to navigate a diabetic renal diet, offering a substitutions guide, cooking techniques, and answers to frequently asked questions.

## DIABETIC RENAL DIET SUBSTITUTIONS GUIDE:

When following a diabetic renal diet, it is crucial to make mindful choices to manage blood sugar levels while supporting kidney health. This substitutions guide offers alternative ingredients that are lower in potassium, phosphorus, and sodium, which are important considerations for individuals with renal conditions.

### POTASSIUM SUBSTITUTIONS:

- Replace high-potassium fruits like bananas and oranges with lower-potassium options such as berries or apples.
- Swap potatoes with cauliflower or green beans as they have lower potassium content.
- Choose low-potassium dairy alternatives like almond milk or coconut milk instead of regular cow's milk.

## PHOSPHORUS SUBSTITUTIONS:

- Opt for lower-phosphorus protein sources like chicken, turkey, or fish instead of high-phosphorus meats such as organ meats or shellfish.
- Use egg whites instead of whole eggs, as the yolk is higher in phosphorus.
- Select lower-phosphorus grains like rice or pasta rather than whole wheat or bran-based products.

## SODIUM SUBSTITUTIONS:

- Use herbs and spices to enhance flavor instead of relying on salt. Experiment with fresh herbs like basil, cilantro, or thyme to add depth to your dishes.
- Choose low-sodium broths, sauces, and condiments to reduce sodium intake.
- Prepare meals from scratch using fresh ingredients to have more control over sodium levels.

## COOKING TECHNIQUES FOR DIABETIC AND RENAL-FRIENDLY MEALS:

Adopting suitable cooking techniques is crucial for individuals following a diabetic renal diet. Here are some recommended methods to maximize flavor while minimizing the use of unhealthy ingredients:

### GRILLING AND ROASTING:

- Grilling and roasting allow you to infuse flavors without adding excessive fats or sodium. Use marinades with diabetic-friendly herbs and spices to add a punch of taste.
- Try grilling lean protein sources like skinless chicken breast or fish fillets, and roast vegetables like zucchini or bell peppers for a healthy and delicious meal.

STEAMING:

- Steaming is an excellent cooking technique to preserve nutrients and natural flavors without adding fats or sodium.
- Steam vegetables like broccoli, carrots, or asparagus to retain their vibrant colors and crisp textures. Steam fish or shellfish for a light and nutritious protein option.

STIR-FRYING:

- Stir-frying is a quick and flavorful cooking technique that requires minimal oil.
- Use heart-healthy oils like olive oil or canola oil sparingly, and load up your stir-fry with an array of colorful vegetables, lean proteins, and diabetic renal-friendly sauces.

FREQUENTLY ASKED QUESTIONS:

CAN I STILL ENJOY FRUITS AND VEGETABLES ON A DIABETIC RENAL DIET?

Yes, you can! It is important to choose fruits and vegetables that are lower in potassium and phosphorus. Refer to the Diabetic Renal Diet Substitutions Guide for suitable options.

## ARE THERE ANY RECOMMENDED COOKING METHODS TO REDUCE PHOSPHORUS IN FOODS?

Soaking and boiling certain high-phosphorus foods can help reduce their phosphorus content. Consult with a registered dietitian or healthcare professional for specific recommendations.

## HOW CAN I MANAGE MY BLOOD SUGAR LEVELS WHILE ALSO CONSIDERING KIDNEY HEALTH?

Balancing carbohydrate intake, monitoring portion sizes, and spreading meals and snacks throughout the day can help manage blood sugar levels. Additionally, following a diabetic renal diet and taking prescribed medications as directed can support kidney health.

## ARE THERE ANY SPECIFIC PRECAUTIONS FOR SEASONING FOOD ON A DIABETIC RENAL DIET?

Excessive salt intake should be avoided. Instead, experiment with herbs, spices, and other flavor enhancers to add depth and taste to your meals without relying on sodium.

Remember, it is essential to consult with a registered dietitian or healthcare professional to personalize your diabetic renal diet based on your individual needs and medical conditions. This appendix serves as a starting point and a resource to support your journey toward a healthy and balanced lifestyle.

(Note: The information provided here is for informational purposes only and should not replace medical advice. Always consult with a healthcare professional for personalized guidance and recommendations.)

# KITCHEN MEASUREMENT
## CONVERSION CHART

### Table 1 - Dry Measurements

| CUPS | TABLESPOON | TEASPOON | OUNCES | MILLILITERS |
|---|---|---|---|---|
| 1/8 | 2 | 6 | 1 | 30 |
| 1/4 | 4 | 12 | 2 | 60 |
| 1/2 | 8 | 24 | 4 | 120 |
| 3/4 | 12 | 36 | 6 | 180 |
| 1 | 16 | 48 | 8 | 240 |

### Table 2 - Liquid Measurements

| GALLON | QUARTS | PINTS | CUPS | OUNCES | LITERS |
|---|---|---|---|---|---|
| 1 | 4 | 8 | 16 | 128 | 3.8 |
| 1/2 | 2 | 4 | 8 | 64 | 1.9 |
| 1/4 | 1 | 2 | 4 | 32 | 0.95 |

### Table 3 - Temperature

| CELSIUS (°C) | FAHRENHEIT (°F) |
|---|---|
| 100 | 212 |
| 130 | 250 |
| 150 | 300 |
| 180 | 350 |
| 200 | 400 |
| 220 | 425 |
| 240 | 475 |

# Table of Contents

Month:

| WEEK | Sun | Mon | Tue | Wed | Thu | Fri | Sat |
|---|---|---|---|---|---|---|---|
| | Date:<br>B:<br>L:<br>D:<br>S: | Date:<br>B:<br>L:<br>D:<br>S: | Date:<br>B:<br>L:<br>D:<br>S: | Date:<br>B:<br>L:<br>D:<br>S: | Date:<br>B:<br>L:<br>D:<br>S: | Date:<br>B:<br>L:<br>D:<br>S: | Date:<br>B:<br>L:<br>D:<br>S: |
| | Date:<br>B:<br>L:<br>D:<br>S: | Date:<br>B:<br>L:<br>D:<br>S: | Date:<br>B:<br>L:<br>D:<br>S: | Date:<br>B:<br>L:<br>D:<br>S: | Date:<br>B:<br>L:<br>D:<br>S: | Date:<br>B:<br>L:<br>D:<br>S: | Date:<br>B:<br>L:<br>D:<br>S: |
| | Date:<br>B:<br>L:<br>D:<br>S: | Date:<br>B:<br>L:<br>D:<br>S: | Date:<br>B:<br>L:<br>D:<br>S: | Date:<br>B:<br>L:<br>D:<br>S: | Date:<br>B:<br>L:<br>D:<br>S: | Date:<br>B:<br>L:<br>D:<br>S: | Date:<br>B:<br>L:<br>D:<br>S: |
| | Date:<br>B:<br>L:<br>D:<br>S: | Date:<br>B:<br>L:<br>D:<br>S: | Date:<br>B:<br>L:<br>D:<br>S: | Date:<br>B:<br>L:<br>D:<br>S: | Date:<br>B:<br>L:<br>D:<br>S: | Date:<br>B:<br>L:<br>D:<br>S: | Date:<br>B:<br>L:<br>D:<br>S: |
| | Date:<br>B:<br>L:<br>D:<br>S: | | | | | | |

B - Breakfast | L - Lunch | D - Dinner | S - Snack

# Table of Contents

Month:

| WEEK | Sun | Mon | Tue | Wed | Thu | Fri | Sat |
|---|---|---|---|---|---|---|---|
|  | Date:<br>B:<br>L:<br>D:<br>S: | Date:<br>B:<br>L:<br>D:<br>S: | Date:<br>B:<br>L:<br>D:<br>S: | Date:<br>B:<br>L:<br>D:<br>S: | Date:<br>B:<br>L:<br>D:<br>S: | Date:<br>B:<br>L:<br>D:<br>S: | Date:<br>B:<br>L:<br>D:<br>S: |
|  | Date:<br>B:<br>L:<br>D:<br>S: | Date:<br>B:<br>L:<br>D:<br>S: | Date:<br>B:<br>L:<br>D:<br>S: | Date:<br>B:<br>L:<br>D:<br>S: | Date:<br>B:<br>L:<br>D:<br>S: | Date:<br>B:<br>L:<br>D:<br>S: | Date:<br>B:<br>L:<br>D:<br>S: |
|  | Date:<br>B:<br>L:<br>D:<br>S: | Date:<br>B:<br>L:<br>D:<br>S: | Date:<br>B:<br>L:<br>D:<br>S: | Date:<br>B:<br>L:<br>D:<br>S: | Date:<br>B:<br>L:<br>D:<br>S: | Date:<br>B:<br>L:<br>D:<br>S: | Date:<br>B:<br>L:<br>D:<br>S: |
|  | Date:<br>B:<br>L:<br>D:<br>S: | Date:<br>B:<br>L:<br>D:<br>S: | Date:<br>B:<br>L:<br>D:<br>S: | Date:<br>B:<br>L:<br>D:<br>S: | Date:<br>B:<br>L:<br>D:<br>S: | Date:<br>B:<br>L:<br>D:<br>S: | Date:<br>B:<br>L:<br>D:<br>S: |
|  | Date:<br>B:<br>L:<br>D:<br>S: |  |  |  |  |  |  |

B – Breakfast | L – Lunch | D – Dinner | S – Snack

# Table of Contents

Month:

| WEEK | Sun | Mon | Tue | Wed | Thu | Fri | Sat |
|---|---|---|---|---|---|---|---|
|  | Date:<br>B:<br>L:<br>D:<br>S: | Date:<br>B:<br>L:<br>D:<br>S: | Date:<br>B:<br>L:<br>D:<br>S: | Date:<br>B:<br>L:<br>D:<br>S: | Date:<br>B:<br>L:<br>D:<br>S: | Date:<br>B:<br>L:<br>D:<br>S: | Date:<br>B:<br>L:<br>D:<br>S: |
|  | Date:<br>B:<br>L:<br>D:<br>S: | Date:<br>B:<br>L:<br>D:<br>S: | Date:<br>B:<br>L:<br>D:<br>S: | Date:<br>B:<br>L:<br>D:<br>S: | Date:<br>B:<br>L:<br>D:<br>S: | Date:<br>B:<br>L:<br>D:<br>S: | Date:<br>B:<br>L:<br>D:<br>S: |
|  | Date:<br>B:<br>L:<br>D:<br>S: | Date:<br>B:<br>L:<br>D:<br>S: | Date:<br>B:<br>L:<br>D:<br>S: | Date:<br>B:<br>L:<br>D:<br>S: | Date:<br>B:<br>L:<br>D:<br>S: | Date:<br>B:<br>L:<br>D:<br>S: | Date:<br>B:<br>L:<br>D:<br>S: |
|  | Date:<br>B:<br>L:<br>D:<br>S: | Date:<br>B:<br>L:<br>D:<br>S: | Date:<br>B:<br>L:<br>D:<br>S: | Date:<br>B:<br>L:<br>D:<br>S: | Date:<br>B:<br>L:<br>D:<br>S: | Date:<br>B:<br>L:<br>D:<br>S: | Date:<br>B:<br>L:<br>D:<br>S: |
|  | Date:<br>B:<br>L:<br>D:<br>S: |  |  |  |  |  |  |

B – Breakfast | L – Lunch | D – Dinner | S – Snack

# Table of Contents

Month:

| WEEK | Sun | Mon | Tue | Wed | Thu | Fri | Sat |
|---|---|---|---|---|---|---|---|
| | Date:<br>B:<br>L:<br>D:<br>S: | Date:<br>B:<br>L:<br>D:<br>S: | Date:<br>B:<br>L:<br>D:<br>S: | Date:<br>B:<br>L:<br>D:<br>S: | Date:<br>B:<br>L:<br>D:<br>S: | Date:<br>B:<br>L:<br>D:<br>S: | Date:<br>B:<br>L:<br>D:<br>S: |
| | Date:<br>B:<br>L:<br>D:<br>S: | Date:<br>B:<br>L:<br>D:<br>S: | Date:<br>B:<br>L:<br>D:<br>S: | Date:<br>B:<br>L:<br>D:<br>S: | Date:<br>B:<br>L:<br>D:<br>S: | Date:<br>B:<br>L:<br>D:<br>S: | Date:<br>B:<br>L:<br>D:<br>S: |
| | Date:<br>B:<br>L:<br>D:<br>S: | Date:<br>B:<br>L:<br>D:<br>S: | Date:<br>B:<br>L:<br>D:<br>S: | Date:<br>B:<br>L:<br>D:<br>S: | Date:<br>B:<br>L:<br>D:<br>S: | Date:<br>B:<br>L:<br>D:<br>S: | Date:<br>B:<br>L:<br>D:<br>S: |
| | Date:<br>B:<br>L:<br>D:<br>S: | Date:<br>B:<br>L:<br>D:<br>S: | Date:<br>B:<br>L:<br>D:<br>S: | Date:<br>B:<br>L:<br>D:<br>S: | Date:<br>B:<br>L:<br>D:<br>S: | Date:<br>B:<br>L:<br>D:<br>S: | Date:<br>B:<br>L:<br>D:<br>S: |
| | Date:<br>B:<br>L:<br>D:<br>S: | | | | | | |

B – Breakfast | L – Lunch | D – Dinner | S – Snack

# Pantry Inventory

Date:

| Item | Quantity | Expiration Date |
|------|----------|-----------------|
| _____ | _____ | _____ |
| _____ | _____ | _____ |
| _____ | _____ | _____ |
| _____ | _____ | _____ |
| _____ | _____ | _____ |
| _____ | _____ | _____ |
| _____ | _____ | _____ |
| _____ | _____ | _____ |
| _____ | _____ | _____ |
| _____ | _____ | _____ |
| _____ | _____ | _____ |
| _____ | _____ | _____ |
| _____ | _____ | _____ |
| _____ | _____ | _____ |
| _____ | _____ | _____ |
| _____ | _____ | _____ |

# Pantry Inventory

Date:

| Item | Quantity | Expiration Date |
|------|----------|-----------------|
|      |          |                 |
|      |          |                 |
|      |          |                 |
|      |          |                 |
|      |          |                 |
|      |          |                 |
|      |          |                 |
|      |          |                 |
|      |          |                 |
|      |          |                 |
|      |          |                 |
|      |          |                 |
|      |          |                 |
|      |          |                 |
|      |          |                 |
|      |          |                 |
|      |          |                 |
|      |          |                 |

# Fridge Inventory

Date:

| Item | Quantity | Expiration Date |
|------|----------|-----------------|
|      |          |                 |
|      |          |                 |
|      |          |                 |
|      |          |                 |
|      |          |                 |
|      |          |                 |
|      |          |                 |
|      |          |                 |
|      |          |                 |
|      |          |                 |
|      |          |                 |
|      |          |                 |
|      |          |                 |
|      |          |                 |
|      |          |                 |
|      |          |                 |

# Fridge Inventory

Date:

| Item | Quantity | Expiration Date |
|------|----------|-----------------|
|      |          |                 |

# Notes

Date:

# Notes

Date:

## Notes

Date:

# Notes

Date:

## Notes

Date:

Printed in Great Britain
by Amazon